Thomas Lovell Beddoes

**Poetical Works**

Edited with a Memoir. Vol. 1

Thomas Lovell Beddoes

**Poetical Works**
*Edited with a Memoir. Vol. 1*

ISBN/EAN: 9783337092849

Printed in Europe, USA, Canada, Australia, Japan

Cover: Foto ©Thomas Meinert / pixelio.de

More available books at **www.hansebooks.com**

# THE
# POETICAL WORKS
OF
# THOMAS LOVELL BEDDOES

EDITED, WITH A MEMOIR, BY
## EDMUND GOSSE
*Hon. M.A. of Trinity College, Cambridge*

*WITH ETCHINGS BY HERBERT RAILTON*

VOL. I.

## LONDON
## J. M. DENT AND CO.
### 69 GREAT EASTERN STREET
1890

THIS EDITION OF THE WORKS OF

BEDDOES

IS DEDICATED BY

THE EDITOR

TO

MRS. ROBERT BARRETT BROWNING

# CONTENTS.

### POEMS HITHERTO UNPUBLISHED.

### THE IMPROVISATORE.

# CONTENTS.

PAGE

Rodolph . . . . . . . . . 212
The Induction to the Third Fytte . . . . 228
Leopold . . . . . . . . . 230

### MISCELLANEOUS POEMS.

The Comet . . . . . . . . . 244
Quatorzains:
    I. To Perfume . . . . . . . 245
    II. Thoughts . . . . . . . 246
    III. A Rivulet . . . . . . . 247
    IV. To Sound . . . . . . . 247
    V. To Night . . . . . . . 248
    VI. A Fantastic Simile . . . . 249
    VII. Another . . . . . . . 250
    VIII. To Silence . . . . . . 250
    IX. To my Lyre . . . . . . 251
    X. To Poesy . . . . . . . 251
    XI. A Clock striking at Midnight . . 252
To a Bunch of Grapes . . . . . . 253

I.                                               *b*

# PREFACE.

URING his own lifetime, with the exception of a few brief contributions to periodicals, Beddoes published nothing but two small volumes. One of these was "The Improvisatore," issued at Oxford in 1821, and so successfully suppressed by its author, that not more than five or six copies are known to exist. It is here reprinted for the first time, from a copy in the collection of Mr. J. Dykes Campbell. The other was "The Brides' Tragedy," published by the Rivingtons in 1822. This is rare, though by no means so inaccessible as its predecessor. A second edition appeared in 1851. It is here reprinted from a copy of the 1822 original in my own library.

At the time of Beddoes' death in 1849 the bulk of his MSS. remained inedited. He specially bequeathed his papers and the disposal of them to Thomas Forbes Kelsall, a solicitor at Fareham, who was the oldest and the most intimate of his English friends. The family of the poet, whose knowledge of him had grown very slight, were at first exceedingly undesirous that his poetic MSS. should be preserved, although they were willing to pay for the publication of any scientific writings. Their repugnance was finally overcome, and in 1850 Kelsall published, in a thin volume, "Death's Jest-Book." The editing of this poem was no light task, for no less than three distinct texts, differing very considerably between themselves, were found to exist. Kelsall collated these three versions, and produced a selected text of his own, to which I have in the main adhered. If the interest in Beddoes should continue to grow, it will always be possible to produce a variorum edition of "Death's Jest-Book," a demand for which, however, is hardly to be expected.

In 1851 Kelsall collected the miscellaneous poems and dramatic fragments into a volume entitled " Poems by the late Thomas Lovell Beddoes." to which he prefixed an anonymous memoir of the poet, which is a model of loving care and respect for the memory of the departed ; a man of whom it might then be said with unusual truth, that he was a bard "whom there were none to praise and very few to love." The result of Kelsall's zeal was that, for the first time, the poetry of Beddoes began to excite attention. Of "Death's Jest-Book " very few copies had been sold, and it is extremely rare in that original condition. The sheets of this and of the " Poems " were rebound, with a new title-page ("The Poems, posthumous and collected, of Thomas Lovell Beddoes"), 1851, in two volumes, to the second of which " The Brides' Tragedy " was added. In this form Beddoes is usually known to collectors, but even these volumes are now difficult to procure. The remainder of them was dispersed by auction in 1855, since which time Beddoes has been out of print.

In 1853 Miss Zoë King, Beddoes' cousin, wrote to Kelsall : "I do not know whether I mentioned to you the high terms of praise with which both Mr. and Mrs. Browning spoke of the poems, just as they were published." Miss Zoë King preserved a romantic interest in T. L. Beddoes, although she, like every other member of his family, knew very little indeed about him personally. She wrote to Kelsall : "I could give you very little information of my early reminiscences of my poor Cousin, as I was so much in awe of his reserve and of his talents that I seldom conversed with him." It was, nevertheless, Miss King for whom Kelsall preserved the highest consideration, and her wishes were consulted in the next step which he took. He had religiously preserved every scrap of Beddoes' writing, and was anxious that these MSS. should be kept together. In consequence of Miss King's report of the admiration which the Brownings felt for Beddoes, and the fact that Robert Browning was the only English poet younger than himself in whom Beddoes took any interest, Kelsall made up his mind to make him the repository of the MSS. But he did not know him. Towards the close, however, of Bryan Waller Procter's life,—I think in 1866 or 1867,—Browning and Kelsall met at his house on one single occasion, and the latter then stated his request.

It is now proper to give the text of the papers by which Kelsall made the transfer of the Beddoes MSS. to Robert Browning :—

"Fareham, *Sept.* 30, 1869.

"It is my wish that after my death, when and so soon as my wife may think proper, the whole of the Beddoes MSS. and papers should be transferred to Mr. Robert Browning, who has consented to accept the charge. It is most desirable, however, that she should look through them and remove the extraneous matter, as there are letters of other people, accounts, etc., which only swell the bulk without increasing the interest. Mr. Browning is to have Miss King's Journal from Switzerland and such of her letters as throw light on Beddoes' life or death. As to the latter, I have considered that my lips were sealed (relating to the suicide) during Miss King's lifetime, since such was her wish, altho' the fact has been communicated to me from an independent source. When my wife and I went to Basle in 1868, we visited Dr. Ecklin (Beddoes' much esteemed physician), and found that he had no doubt as to the injuries which brought Beddoes to the Hospital having been self-inflicted, and that accident there was none.

"He saw a good deal of Beddoes during his stay at the Hospital before and after the amputation, and considered that in all their communications the origin of his situation was an understood fact between them. Dr. Ecklin added the startling information that the final catastrophe was, in his opinion, the direct result of a self-administered poison—all the symptoms being otherwise wholly unaccountable, and corresponding to those appropriate to the application of a very strong poison called Kurara or [blank in MS.]. He was evidently tired of life, and the fact of his being so, and of having achieved his release, need not, after a fair allowance for family hesitation, and in my opinion should not, be withheld from the knowledge of those who take a deep and true interest in Beddoes as a great poet.

"THOS. F. KELSALL."

To this paper succeeded another :—

"I transfer to Robert Browning all my interests and authority in and over the MSS. and papers of or concerning the poet Beddoes, for him to act discretionally for the honour of the poet.

"The greater portion of these MSS. was *given* by him to me in his life-time, and the remainder placed at my absolute disposal by his death-bed memorandum.

"T. F. KELSALL.

"Fareham, *June* 15, '72."

Shortly after this Mr. Kelsall died, and the box containing the Beddoes papers was transmitted to Mr. Robert Browning. They remained locked up and unexamined until, in July, 1883, Mr. Browning invited me to help him in undertaking a complete investigation of the MSS. When we had reduced them to some order, he lent them to me, and I made such transcripts and collations as have formed the basis of the present edition. With regard to the circumstances of Beddoes' death, which are now for the first time made public, it was Mr. Browning's wish that Kelsall's instructions should be followed, at a proper interval after the death of Miss Zoë King, who was the last person to whom the statement could give any personal pain. Miss King died on Sept. 28, 1881, and I therefore judge that the time has arrived for carrying out Kelsall's directions.

The Beddoes Papers remain in the possession of Mr. Robert Barrett Browning, who has very kindly lent them to me again, that I might revise my collation. In the preparation of these volumes I have received invaluable aid from my friend Mr. J. Dykes Campbell, who is unequalled and perhaps unapproached in his knowledge of the late Georgian period of English poetical history.

E. G.

# THOMAS LOVELL BEDDOES.

## INTRODUCTION.

### I.

IN a letter written to Kelsall in 1824, Beddoes makes the following remarks on the poetical situation of the moment :—

"The disappearance of Shelley from the world seems, like the tropical setting of that luminary to which his poetical genius can alone be compared, with reference to the companions of his day, to have been followed by instant darkness and owl-season ; whether the vociferous Darley is to be the comet, or tender full-faced L. E. L. the milk-and-watery moon of our darkness, are questions for the astrologers ; if I were the literary weather-guesser for 1825 I would safely prognosticate fog, rain, blight in due succession for its dullard months."

When these words were written, the death of Byron four months previously had closed, for English readers, a romantic phase of our national verse. If Keats, Shelley, and Byron, however, were gone, it may be objected that all the other great poets of the age survived. This is true in a physical sense,

but how many of them were still composing verse
of any brilliant merit? Not Coleridge, long ago
stricken dumb to verse; not Wordsworth, prosing
on without the stimulus of inspiration; even
Moore or Southey were vocal no longer; Campbell
and Scott had practically taken farewell of the
Muse. English poetry had been in blossom from
1795 to 1820, but the marvellous bloom was over,
and the petals were scattered on the grass.

The subject of this memoir began to write at the
very moment of complete exhaustion, when the age
was dazzled with excess of genius, and when the
nation was taking breath for a fresh burst of song.
He had the misfortune to be a young man when
Keats and Shelley were just dead, and when
Tennyson and Browning were schoolboys. In the
words which have just been quoted he has given a
humorous view of the time, which shows that, at
the age of twenty-one, he had grasped its character-
istics. Among his exact contemporaries there was no
one, except Praed, who was some months his senior,
who inherited anything like genius. Beddoes was
four years younger than Hood, two years older
than Elizabeth Barrett. No other name has survived worthy of being even named beside his as a
poet, except Macaulay, with whom he has nothing
in common. He was early dissuaded from the
practice of verse, and all that he has left, which is
of any sterling value, was composed between 1821,
when he published "The Improvisatore," and 1826,
when he practically finished "Death's Jest-Book."
He belongs to those five years of exhaustion and
mediocrity, and the effect of having to write at

such a period, there can be no doubt, dwarfed, restrained, and finally quenched his poetical faculty. It is not saying much, yet it is mere justice to insist, that Beddoes was, during those five years, the most interesting talent engaged in writing English verse.

## II.

Thomas Lovell Beddoes was born in Rodney place, Clifton, on the 20th of July, 1803. He was the eldest son of a celebrated physician, Dr. Thomas Beddoes, who died in 1809, and left his son to the guardianship of Davies Giddy, afterwards known as Sir Davies Gilbert, P.R.S., who lived for thirty years longer. The boy's mother, Anna, was a sister of Maria Edgeworth, the novelist. He was educated at Bath Grammar School and at the Charterhouse, where, as early as 1817, he began to write verses. Of his character at school, where he showed signs at once of that eccentricity and independence of manners which were to distinguish him through life, a schoolfellow, Mr. C. D. Bevan, has preserved a very entertaining account, from which this short extract may be given:—

"He knew Shakespeare well when I first saw him, and during his stay at the Charterhouse made himself master of all the best English dramatists, from Shakespeare's time, or before it, to the plays of the day. He liked acting, and was a good judge of it, and used to give apt though burlesque imitations of the popular actors, particularly of Kean and Macready. Though his voice was harsh and his enunciation offensively conceited, he read with so much propriety of expression and manner that I was always glad to listen : even when I was pressed into the service as his accomplice, or his enemy, or his love, with a due accompaniment of curses, caresses, or kicks, as the course of his declamation required.   One play in particular, Marlow's tragedy of ' Dr. Faustus,' excited my admiration, and was fixed on my memory in this way."

At school he came under the influence of Fielding, and wrote a novel, entitled "Cynthio and Bugboo," the loss of which we need scarcely deplore, as, according to the same authority, it was marked by "all the coarseness, little of the wit, and none of the truth of his original." The fragments of his schoolboy verse, in particular the rhapsody of "Alfarabi," display a very singular adroitness in the manufacture of easy blank verse, and precocious tendency to a species of mocking metaphysics, both equally unlike a child.  In July, 1819, while still at Charterhouse, a sonnet of his was printed in the "Morning Post."  On the 1st of May, 1820, Beddoes proceeded to Oxford, and was entered a commoner at Pembroke, which had been his father's college.

Although he had been a forward boy at school, Beddoes passed through Oxford without any academic distinction.  He was a freshman of eighteen when, in 1821, he published his first volume, "The Improvisatore," of which he afterwards carefully tried to destroy every copy.  In 1822 he published, as another thin pamphlet, "The Brides' Tragedy," which has also become extremely rare.  These two little books, the work of an undergraduate less than twenty years of age, are the only ones which Beddoes ever published. The remainder of his writings, whether lyrical or dramatic, were issued posthumously, not less than thirty years later. "The Brides' Tragedy" attracted some notice in literary circles; it secured for the young Oxford poet the friendship of a man much older than himself, but of kindred tastes, Bryan Waller Procter. The dramatic poems of "Barry Cornwall," of which "Mirandola" was then the latest, had been appearing in rapid succession, and their amiable author was a person of considerable influence. It was Procter who, in 1823, introduced Beddoes to Thomas Forbes Kelsall, a young lawyer practising at Southampton. It had been thought well that Beddoes, who was sadly behind-hand with his studies, should go down to this quiet town to read for his bachelor's degree, and he remained at Southampton for some months, in great intimacy with Kelsall, and forming no other acquaintance.

While he was at Southampton, Beddoes wrote a great deal of desultory verse, almost all of a dramatic order; to this period belong "The Second Brother" and "Torrismond," among other fragments. Already he was seized with that inability to finish, that lack of an organic principle of poetical composition, which were to prevent him from mounting to those heights of which his facility and brilliancy seem to promise him an easy ascent. The death of Shelley appears to have drawn his attention to the genius of that writer, by which he was instantly fascinated, and, as it were, absorbed.

Outside the small circle of Shelley's personal
friends, Beddoes was perhaps the first to appre-
ciate the magnitude of his merit, as he was certainly the earliest to imitate Shelley's lyrical work.
His letters to Procter and Kelsall are full of evi-
dence of his over-mastering passion for Shelley,
and it was to Beddoes, in the first instance, that
the publication of that writer's "Posthumous
Poems" was due.   In the winter of 1823 Beddoes
started a subscription with his two friends, and
corresponded with John Hunt on the subject.  They
promised to take 250 copies, but Hunt said that
Mrs. Shelley ought to have some profit.   This
seemed hardly fair to Beddoes; "for the twinkling
of this very distant chance we, three poor honest
admirers of Shelley's poetry, are certainly to pay."
At this time Beddoes was writing two romantic
dramas, "Love's Arrow Poisoned" and "The
Last Man," both founded on the tragic model of
Webster, Cyril Tourneur, and Middleton.   Of
these plays not very much was ever written, and
still less is now in existence.  Of "The Last Man"
he writes, in February 1824: "There are now three
first acts in my drawer.   When I have got two
more, I shall stitch them together, and stick the
sign of a fellow tweedling a mask in his fingers,
with 'good entertainment for man and ass' understood."

The year 1824 he spent in London, Oxford, and
Bristol.   Already his eccentric shyness had grown
upon him.   He writes to Kelsall from his lodgings
in Devereux Court, Temple, March 29, 1824:—

"Being a little shy and not a little proud perhaps, I have held back and never made the first step towards discovering my residence or existence to any of my family friends [in London]. In consequence I have lived in a deserted state, which I could hardly bear much longer without sinking into that despondency on the brink of which I have sate so long. Your cheerful presence at times (could we not mess together occasionally?) would set me up a good deal, but perhaps you had better not draw my heavy company on your head. . . . . I met an intelligent man who had lived at Hampstead, seen Keats, and was read in his and the poems of Shelley. On my mentioning the former by accident to him, he complimented me on my similarity of countenance; he did not think much of K.'s genius, and therefore did not say it insincerely or sycophantically. The same was said by Procter and Taylor before."

Mrs. Procter, who had known both poets, made the same remark about Beddoes to myself; but she added that she never saw in the latter the extraordinary look of inspiration which was ocasionally to be detected in the great eyes of Keats.

In the summer of 1824 Beddoes was hastily called to Florence by the illness of his mother, who was living there. She died before he could reach her, but he spent some weeks there, saw Walter Savage Landor, and then returned to Clifton in charge of his sisters. In October of the same year he began to study German, a language then but little known in this country. He attacked it languidly at first, then with ever-increasing eagerness and zest. But the Elizabethan drama was still his principal delight, and he studied it, even in its least illustrious forms, with extraordinary close-ness and delight. Writing to Kelsall from Clifton (January 11, 1825), he remarks, apropos of a revival of "The Fatal Dowry" of Massinger:—

"Say what you will, I am convinced the man who is to awaken the drama must be a bold tramp-ling fellow—no creeper into worm-holes—no reviver even, however good. These reanimations are vampire-cold. Such ghosts as Marloe, Webster, etc., are better dramatists, better poets, I dare say, than any contemporary of ours, but they are ghosts—the worm is in their pages,—and we want to see something that our great-grandsires did not know. With the greatest reverence for all the antiquities of the drama, I still think that we had better beget than revive, attempt to give the litera-ture of this age an idiosyncracy and spirit of its own, and only raise a ghost to gaze on, not to live with. Just now the drama is a haunted ruin. I am glad that you are awakening to a sense of Darley. He must have no little perseverance to have gone through so much of that play; it will perchance be the first star of a new day."

The result of so much meditation on the drama was the composition of more fragments. "The Second Brother," "Torrismond," and "The Last Man" occupied Beddoes during the winter and spring of 1824-5. But none of these approached completion. He then planned the publication of a volume of lyrics, to be entitled "Outidana, or Effusions, amorous, pathetic, and fantastical," which was to include most of the miscellaneous verses reprinted in this edition, and others which are now lost. On the 25th of May, 1825, he took an ordinary bachelor's degree at Oxford. He writes to Kelsall from Pembroke College, on the 8th of June, announcing for the first time the most celebrated of his writings :—

"Oxford is the most indolent place on earth. I have fairly done nothing in the world but read a play or two of Schiller, Æschylus and Euripides, —you I suppose read German now as fast as English. I do not finish that 2nd Brother you saw but am thinking of a very Gothic-styled tragedy for which I have a jewel of a name :—

DEATH'S JESTBOOK—

of course no one will ever read it. Mr. Milman (our poetry professor) has made me quite unfashionable here by denouncing me as one of a ' villainous school.' I wish him another son."

He now suddenly determined to abandon literature, which had suggested itself to him as a profession, and take up the study of medicine. We find him, therefore, on the 19th of July, 1825, at Hamburg, "sitting on a horse-hair sofa, looking over the Elbe, with his meerschaum at his side, full of Grave, and abundantly prosaic. To-morrow, according to the prophecies of the diligence, he will set out for Hanover, and by the end of this week mein Herr Thomas will probably be a Doctor of the university of Göttingen." This, however, was rather premature. He did not become a doctor until much later. It is important to observe that the exodus to Germany thus casually and nonchalantly taken involved nothing less, as it proved, than a complete alteration in all his habits. Except for very few and brief visits, he did not return to England for the rest of his life, and he so completely adopted the language and thoughts of a German student as almost to cease to be an Englishman.

At Göttingen the celebrated man of science, Prof. Blumenbach, became the most intimate friend of Beddoes. The latter threw himself with the utmost ardour into the study of physiology and medicine. He did not, however, at first abandon his design of becoming an English dramatic poet. He writes to Kelsall (Dec. 4, 1825) :—

"I am perhaps somewhat independent, and have a competence adequate to my philosophical desires. There are reasons why I should reject too much practice if it did intrude; really I am much more likely to remain a patientless physician. And now I will end this unnecessary subject, by telling you that 'Death's Jestbook' goes on like the tortoise, slow and sure; I think it will be entertaining, very unamiable, and utterly unpopular. Very likely it may be finished in the spring or autumn."

His misanthropy, for it almost deserves so harsh a name, grew upon him. "I feel myself," he wrote, "in a measure alone in the world and likely to remain so, for, from the experiments I have made, I fear I am a non-conductor of friendship, a not-very-likeable person, so that I must make sure of my own respect, and occupy that part of the brain which should be employed in imaginative attachments in the pursuit of immaterial and unchanging good." In April, 1826, "Death's Jest-Book" is still lying "like a snow-ball, and I give it a kick every now and then, out of mere scorn and ill-humour ; the 4th act, and I may say the 5th are more than half done, so that at last it will be a perfect mouse, but such doggerell ! " None the less did he anticipate that the poem would come "like an electric shock among the small critics." In October, 1826, it is "done and done for, its limbs being as scattered and unconnected as those of the old gentleman whom Medea minced and boiled young. I have tried 20 times at least to copy it fair." He intended at this time to send the MS. to Kelsall and Procter to be seen through the press, but he delayed until he could bring the poem himself to London.

His monotonous existence in Göttingen was broken in the spring of 1828 by a visit of a few days to England, where he took his degree of M.A. at Oxford, and hurried back to Germany. Meanwhile he had left "Death's Jest-Book" with Procter and Kelsall for publication, but they decided that it must be "revised and improved." In his fifth year in Germany, "having already been at Göttingen the time which it is allowed for any student to remain there," he transferred his residence to Würzburg, in Bavaria ; "a very clever professor of medicine and capital midwife brought me here, and a princely hospital." In 1831 there was again some abortive talk of publishing "Death's Jest-Book." About this time Beddoes became more and more affected by opinions of the extreme radi-

cal order ; he subscribed towards " the support of
candidates who were professed supporters of the
Reform Bill," and he began to affect a warm personal interest in certain revolutionary Poles who had
taken up their abode in Würzburg. He continued
his medical studies with great thoroughness, and
in the summer of 1832 he took his degree of
doctor of medicine in the university, being now in
his thirtieth year. He was more and more mixed
up in political intrigue, and on the 25th of September, 1832, he somewhat obscurely says :—

" The absurdity of the King of Bavaria has cost
me a good deal, as I was obliged to oppose every
possible measure to the arbitrary illegality of his
conduct, more for the sake of future objects of his
petty royal malice than my own, of course in vain."

He was soon after obliged to fly, " banished by
that ingenious Jackanapes of Bavaria," in common
with several of his distinguished Würzburg friends.
He took refuge, first in Strassburg, then in Zurich.
He brought with him to Switzerland a considerable
reputation as a physiologist, for Blumenbach, in a
testimonial which exists, calls him the best pupil
he ever had. It appears that he now assumed,
what he afterwards dropped, the degree of M.D.,
and had some practice as a physician in the town of
Zurich. In 1835 the surgeon Schoenlien proposed
Beddoes to the medical faculty of the University as
professor of Comparative Anatomy, and the latter
unanimously seconded him. His election, however,
was not ratified, according to one of his letters,
for political reasons, according to another because
he was found to be ineligible, from his having pub-

lished nothing of a medical character. He spent several healthy and tolerably happy years in Zurich, "what," he says in March, 1837, "with a careless temper and the pleasant translunary moods I walk and row myself into upon the lakes and over the Alps of Switzerland"; and once more, as he quaintly put it, he began "to brew small ale out with the water of the fountain of the horse's foot," working again on the revision of "Death's Jest-Book." He also began to prepare for the press a collection of his narrative and lyrical poems, to be called "The Ivory Gate." In 1838 he was engaged in translating Grainger's work on the Spinal Cord into German.

He had spent six years at Zurich, and was beginning to feel that city to have become his settled home, when, on the 8th of September, 1839, a political catastrophe destroyed his peace of mind. A mob of six thousand peasants, "half of them unarmed, and the other half armed with scythes, dung-forks and poles, led on by a mad fanatic and aided by some traitors in the cabinet, and many in the town," stormed Zurich, and upset the liberal government of the canton. Beddoes observed the riot from a window, and witnessed the murder of the minister Hegetoch-weiber, who was one of his best friends. He wrote: "In consequence of this state of things, in which neither property nor person is secure, I shall find it necessary to give up my present residence entirely. Indeed, the dispersion of my friends and acquaintance, all of whom belonged to the liberal party, renders it nearly impossible for me to remain longer here." He loitered on, however,

until March, 1840, when his life was threatened by
the insurgents, and he was helped to fly from Zurich
in secret by a former leader of the liberal party, whom
he had befriended, a man of the name of Jasper.

It is probable that the seven years Beddoes
spent at Zurich formed the happiest portion of his
life. He was never to experience tranquillity
again. The next few years were spent in what
seems an aimless wandering through the length
and breadth of Central Europe. Little is known
of his history from this time forward. In 1841 he
was in Berlin, where he formed an acquaintance-
ship with a young Dr. Frey, who remained his
intimate friend to the last. In 1842 he made
a brief visit to England. In 1843 he went to
Baden in Aargau, where he seems to have stored
his library, and, so far as Beddoes henceforth could
be said to have a home, that home was in this little
town of Northern Switzerland, not far from Zurich.
He spent the winter of 1844 at Giessen, attracted
thither by Liebig and his famous school of chemis-
try, after having lodged through the summer and
autumn at Basel, Strassburg, Mannheim, Mainz,
and Frankfurt in succession. At Giessen a little
of the poetic fervour returned to him, and it was
here that he wrote " The Swallow leaves her Nest "
and "In Lover's Ear a wild Voice cried." But most
of his verse now was written in German. He says
(Nov. 13, 1844) : "Sometimes to amuse myself
I write a German lyric or epigram, right scurrilous,
many of which have appeared in the Swiss and
German papers, and some day or other I shall have
them collected and printed for fun." It is needless to

say that he never issued this collection, and the German poems, doubtless signed with a pseudonym or else anonymous, have never been traced.

In August, 1846, he came to England for a considerable stay. Intending to remain six weeks, he loitered on for ten months. His friends, few of whom had seen him for more than twenty years, found him altered beyond all recognition. He had become extremely rough and cynical in speech, and eccentric in manners. I am informed by a member of his family that he arrived at the residence of one of his relations, Cheney Longville, near Ludlow, astride the back of a donkey. He complained of neuralgia, and for six out of the ten months which he spent in England, he was shut up in a bedroom, reading and smoking, and admitting no visitor. In April, 1847, he went down to Fareham, to stay with Mr. Kelsall, and this greatly brightened him up. From Fareham he proceeded in May to London, and there he met with his old friends the Procters. From Mrs. Procter the present writer received a graphic account of his manners and appearance. She told me that his eccentricities were so marked that they almost gave the impression of insanity, but that closer observation showed them to be merely the result of a peculiar fancy, entirely unaccustomed to restraint, and of the occasional rebound of spirits after a period of depression. The Procters found Beddoes a most illusive companion. He would come to them uninvited, but never if he had been asked, or if he feared to meet a stranger. On one occasion, Mrs. Procter told me, they had asked Beddoes to dine with them, and proceed

afterwards to Drury Lane Theatre. He did not
come, and they dined alone. On approaching
the theatre, they saw Beddoes in charge of the
police, and on inquiry found that he had just been
arrested for trying to put Drury Lane on fire.
The incendiary, however, had used no more dangerous torch than a five-pound note, and Mr.
Procter had little difficulty in persuading the
police that this was much more likely to hurt the
pocket of Mr. Beddoes than the rafters of the
theatre.

In June, 1847, Beddoes returned to Frankfurt,
where he lived until the spring of 1848 with a
baker named Degen, who was then about nine-
teen years of age,—"a nice-looking young man
dressed in a blue blouse, fine in expression, and
of a natural dignity of manner," Miss Zoë King
describes him. While Beddoes was in Frankfurt
his blood became poisoned from the virus of a
dead body entering a slight wound in his hand.
This was overcome, but it greatly weakened and
depressed him. For six months he would see no
one but Degen. He complained of disgust of life,
and declared that his republican friends in Germany
had deserted him. He persuaded Degen to become an actor, and he occupied himself in teaching
him English and other accomplishments, cutting
himself off from all other company. At this time
"he had let his beard grow, and looked like
Shakespeare." In May, 1848, he left Frankfurt,
inducing Degen to accompany him, and the two
companions wandered together through Germany
and Switzerland. In Zurich Beddoes chartered the

theatre for one night, to give his friend an opportunity of appearing in the part of Hotspur. For about six weeks, so far as it is possible to discover, Beddoes was tolerably happy. But he was separated from Degen at Basel, where Beddoes took a room, in a condition of dejected apathy that was pitiful to witness, at the Cicogne Hôtel. Here very early next morning he inflicted a deep wound on his right leg, with a razor. "Il etait miserable,—il a voula se tuer," as the waiter who attended upon him said afterwards to Miss Zoë King. He was, however, removed with success to the Town Hospital, where his friends Dr. Frey and Dr. Ecklin waited upon him. He had a pleasant private room, looking into a large garden. He communicated with his English friends, being very anxious to allay all suspicion. He wrote to his sister: "In July I fell with a horse in a precipitous part of the neighbouring hills, and broke my left leg all to pieces." He begged no one in England to be anxious, and his version of the catastrophe was accepted without question. The leg, however, was obstinate in recovery, for the patient stealthily tore off the bandages, and eventually gangrene of the foot set in. On the 9th of September it became necessary to amputate the leg below the knee-joint; this operation was very successfully performed by Dr. Ecklin. Beddoes seems to have been cheerful during the autumn months, and Degen came back to Basel, lodging near him in the town. The poet gave up all suicidal attempts, and it was considered that his mind on this matter was completely cured. His bed was covered with books, and he conversed and wrote

freely about literature and science.  He talked of
going to Italy when he was convalescent, and in
December he walked out of his room twice.  The
first time he went out into the town, however, on
the 26th of January, 1849, he seems to have used
his authority as a physician to procure the deadly
poison called Kurara ; in the course of the evening
Dr. Ecklin was suddenly called to his bedside, and
found the poet lying on his back insensible, with
the following extraordinary note, written in pencil,
folded on his bosom.  It was addressed to one of the
oldest of his English friends, Mr. R. Phillips :—

" MY DEAR PHILLIPS,
    " I am food for what I am good for—worms.
I have made a will here, which I desire to be
respected ; and add the donation of £20 to Dr.
Ecklin my physician.  Thanks for all kindnesses.
Borrow the £200.  You are a good and noble
man, and your children must look sharp to be like
you.
                " Yours, if my own, ever
                            "T. L. B.

    " Love to Anna, Henry,—the Beddoes of Long-
vile and Zoë and Emmeline King.  Also to Kelsall,
whom I beg to look at my MSS. and print or not
as *he* thinks fit.  I ought to have been, [among a]
variety of other things, a good poet.  Life was too
great a bore on one peg, and that a bad one.
W. Beddoes must have a case (50 bottles) of
Champagne Moet 1847 growth.  Buy for Dr.
Ecklin above mentioned Reade's best stomach-
pump."

He died at 10 p.m. the same night, and was buried under a cypress in the cemetery of the hospital. The circumstances of his death, now for the first time published, were ascertained by Miss Zoë King, who visited Basel in 1857, and saw Degen, Frey, Ecklin, and the people at the Cicogne Hôtel. After some delay, the various MSS. of Beddoes were placed in Kelsall's hands, and that faithful and admirable friend published the version of "Death's Jest-Book," which seemed to him the most attractive, in 1850; and this he followed, in 1851, by the "Miscellaneous Poems," with an unsigned Memoir. These two volumes form the only monument hitherto raised to the memory of the unfortunate poet. The reception which was given to them was respectful, and even sympathetic. It may be sufficient here to give one instance of it, which has never been made public. Miss Zoë King, in a letter to Kelsall, says: "I was at the Lakes with my uncle Edgeworth just after receiving the 'Death's Jest-Book,' and was very much pleased to lend it to Mr. Tennyson. He was just arrived (and at a distance from us) on his wedding tour, so that I merely *saw* him. He returned the book with a few lines . . . rating it highly."

## III.

It is not in the fragments that Beddoes has left behind him that we can look for the work of a full-orbed and serene poetical genius. It would be a narrow definition indeed of the word "poet" which should exclude him, but he belongs to the secondary

order of makers.   He is not one of those whose
song flows unbidden from their lips, those born
warblers whom neither poverty, nor want of
training, nor ignorance, can restrain from tuneful
utterance.   He belongs to the tribe of scholar-
poets, to the educated artists in verse.   In every
line that he wrote we can trace the influence of
existing verse upon his mind.   He is intellectual
rather than spontaneous.   Nor, even within this
lower range, does his work extend far on either
hand.   He cultivates a narrow field, and his im-
pressions of life and feeling are curiously limited
and monotonous.   At the feast of the Muses he
appears bearing little except one small savoury
dish, some cold preparation, we may say, of olives
and anchovies, the strangeness of which has to
make up for its lack of importance.   Not every
palate enjoys this *hors d'œuvre*, and when that is
the case, Beddoes retires; he has nothing else to
give.   He appeals to a few literary epicures, who,
however, would deplore the absence of this oddly
flavoured dish as much as that of any more important *pièce de resistance.*

As a poet, the great defect of Beddoes has
already been alluded to,—his want of sustained
invention, his powerlessness in evolution.   He was
poor just where, two hundred years earlier, almost
every playwright in the street had been strong,
namely, in the ability to conduct an interesting
story to a thrilling and appropriate close.   From
this point of view his boyish play, "The Brides'
Tragedy," is his only success.   In this case a story
was developed with tolerable skill to a dramatic

ending. But, with one exception, he never again could contrive to drag a play beyond a certain point; in the second or third act its wings would droop, and it would expire, do what its master would. These unfinished tragedies were like those children of Polynesian dynasties, anxiously trained, one after another, in the warm Pacific air, yet ever doomed to fall, on the borders of manhood, by the breath of the same mysterious disease. " Death's Jest-Book " is but an apparent exception. This does indeed appear in the guise of a finished five-act play ; but its completion was due to the violent determination of its author, and not to legitimate inspiration. For many years, in and out of season, Beddoes, who had pledged his whole soul to the finishing of this book, assailed it with all the instruments of his art, and at last produced a huge dramatic Frankenstein, which, by adroit editing, could be forced into the likeness of a tragedy. But no play in literature was less of a spontaneous creation, or was further from achieving the ideal of growing like a tree.

From what Beddoes was not, however, it is time to pass to what he was. In several respects, then, he was a poetical artist of consummate ability. Of all the myriad poets and poeticules who have tried to recover the lost magic of the tragic blank verse of the Elizabethans, Beddoes has come nearest to success. If it were less indifferent to human interests of every ordinary kind, the beauty of his dramatic verse would not fail to fascinate. To see how strong it is, how picturesque, how admirably fashioned, we have only to compare it with what others have done in the same style, with the tragic verse, for instance, of Barry Cornwall, of Talfourd, of Horne. But Beddoes is what he himself has called "a creeper into worm-holes." He attempts nothing personal; he follows the very tricks of Marston and Cyril Tourneur like a devoted disciple. The passions with which he invariably deals are remote and unfamiliar; we may go further, and say that they are positively obsolete. In another place I have compared Beddoes in poetry with the Helsche Breughel in painting. He dedicates himself to the service of Death, not with a brooding sense of the terror and shame of mortality, but from a love of the picturesque pageantry of it, the majesty and sombre beauty, the swift, theatrical transitions, the combined elegance and horror that wait upon the sudden decease of monarchs. His medical taste and training encouraged this tendency to dwell on the physical aspects of death, and gave him a sort of ghastly familiarity with images drawn from the bier and the charnel-house. His attitude, however, though cold and cynical, was always distinguished, and in his wildest flights of humour he escapes vulgarity. In this he shows himself a true poet. As we read his singular pages, we instinctively expect to encounter the touch of prose which, in Landor's phrase, will precipitate the whole, yet it never comes. Beddoes often lacks inspiration, but distinction he can never be said to lack.

As a lyrist he appears, on the whole, to rank higher than as a dramatist. Several of his songs, artificial as they are, must always live, and take a high place in the literature of artifice. As a writer of this class of poem his experience of the Elizabethans was further kindled and largely modified by the example of Shelley. Nevertheless his finest songs could never be taken for the work of Shelley, or, indeed, attributed to any hand but his own. Among them, the song in "Torrismond" is perhaps the sweetest and the most ingenious; "Dream-Pedlary" the most exquisite. The "Song of the Stygian Naiades" and "Old Adam, the Carrion Crow" are instances of fancy combined with grisly humour, of a class in which Beddoes has no English competitor. The Harpagus ballad in the fourth act of "Death's Jest-Book," and "Lord Alcohol," which is here for the first time printed, are less known, but no less vivid and extraordinary. Beddoes possesses great sense of verbal melody, a fastidious ear, and considerable, though far from faultless, skill in metrical architecture. His boyish volume, called "The Improvisatore," which is here presented to the readers of Beddoes practically for the first time, shows, despite its crudity, that these gifts were early developed. To say more in this place is needless. Those readers who are able to take pleasure in poetry so grim, austere, and abnormal, may safely be left to discover its specific charms for themselves.

EDMUND GOSSE.

POEMS COLLECTED IN 1851

[Of the poems in this section three were printed during the life of Beddoes. "The Romance of the Lily" was published in "The Album" for August, 1823. In the "Athenæum" were printed "Love's Last Messages" (July 7, 1832), and "Lines written in 'Prometheus Unbound'" (May 18, 1833). The remainder were first published by Kelsall in 1851. Wherever the present text differs from his, it has been modified by reference to the original MSS. I have retained most of the titles invented by Kelsall.]

# ALFARABI;

## THE WORLD-MAKER.

### A RHAPSODICAL FRAGMENT.

'WAS in those days
    That never were, nor ever shall be,
       reader,
    But on this paper; golden, glorious
  days,
Such as the sun, (poor fellow! by the way,
Where is he? I've not seen him all this winter,)—
Never could spin : days, as I said before,
Which shall be made as fine as ink can make them ;
So, clouds, avaunt ! and Boreas, hence ! to blow
Old Ætna's porridge.   We will make the sun
Rise, like a gentleman, at noon ; clasped round
With the bright armour of his May-day beams ;
The summer-garland on his beaming curls, ·
With buds of palest brightness ; and one cloud—
Yes, (I'm an Englishman,) one snow-winged cloud,
To wander slowly down the trembling blue ;
A wind that stops and pants along the grass,
Trembles and flies again, like thing pursued ;

And indescribable, delightful sounds,
Which dart along the sky, we know not whence;
Bees we must have to hum, shrill-noted swallows
With their small, lightning wings, to fly about,
And tilt against the waters :—that will do.
And now, dear climate, only think what days
I'd make if you'd employ me : you should have
A necklace, every year, of such as this ;
Each bead of the three hundred sixty five—
(Excuse me, puss, (&) I couldn't get you in,)
Made up of sunshine, moonshine, and blue skies :
Starlight I'd give you in :—but where are we ?
I see : 'twas in those days that Alfarabi lived ;
A man renowned in the newspapers :
He wrote in two reviews ; raw pork at night
He ate, and opium ; kept a bear at college :
A most extraordinary man was he.
But he was one not satisfied with man,
As man has made himself : he thought this life
Was something deeper than a jest, and sought
Into its roots : himself was his best science.
He touched the springs, the unheeded hiero-
    glyphics
Deciphered ; like an antiquary sage
Within an house of office, which he takes
For druid temple old, here he picked up
A tattered thought, and turned it o'er and o'er
'Till it was spelled ; the names of all the tenants,
Pencilled upon the wall, he would unite ;
Until he found the secret and the spell
Of life.   'Twas not by Logic, reader ;
Her and her crabbed sister, Metaphysics,
Left he to wash Thought's shirt, the shirt bemired

On that proverbial morning. By his own mind,
The lamp that never fails us, dared we trust it,
He read the mystery; and it was one
To the dull sense of common man unknown,
Incomprehensible; a miracle
Of magic, yet as true and obvious,
For thoughtful ones to hit on, as the sun.
He knew the soul would free itself in sleep
From her dull sister, bear itself away,
Freer than air: to guide it with his will,
To bear his mortal sight and memory,
On these excursions, was the power he found.
He found it, and he used it. For, one night,
By the internal vision he saw Sleep,
Just after dinner, tapping at the door
Of his next neighbour, the old alderman.
Sleep rode a donkey with a pair of wings,
And, having fastened its ethereal bridle
Unto the rails, walked in. Now, Alfarabi!
Leap, Alfarabi! There! the saddle's won:
He kicks, he thwacks, he spurs,—the donkey flies.
On soared they, like the bright thought of an eye,
'Mid the infinity of elements.
First through the azure meads of night and day,
Among the rushing of the million flames,
They passed the bearded dragon-star, unchained
From Hell, (of old its sun,) yelling her way
Upon those wings, compact of mighty clouds
Bloodshot and black, or flaring devilish light,
Whose echo racks the shrieking universe,
Whose glimpse is tempest. O'er each silent star
Slept like a tomb that dark, marmoreal bird,
That spell-bound ocean, Night,—her breast o'erwrit

With golden secresies.   All these he passed,
One after one : as he, who stalks by night,
With the ghost's step, the shaggy murderer
Leaves passed the dreamy city's sickly lamps.
Then through the horrid twilight did they plunge,
The universe's suburbs ; dwelling dim
Of all that sin and suffer ; midnight shrieks
Upon the water, when no help is near ;
The blood-choaked curse of him who dies in bed
By torch-light, with a dagger in his heart ;
The parricidal and incestuous laugh ;
And the last cries of those whom devils hale
Quick into hell ; deepened the darkness.
And there were sounds of wings, broken and swift ;
Blows of wrenched poniards, muffled in thick flesh ;
Struggles and tramplings wild, splashes and falls,
And inarticulate yells from human breasts.
Nought was beheld : but Alfarabi's heart
Turned in his bosom, like a scorched leaf,
And his soul faded.   When again he saw,
His steed had paused.   It was within a space
Upon the very boundary and brim
Of the whole universe, the outer edge
Which seemed almost to end the infinite zone ;
A chasm in the almighty thoughts, forgotten
By the omnipotent ; a place apart,
Like some great, ruinous dream of broken worlds
Tumbling through heaven, or Tartarus' panting jaws
Open above the sun.   Sky was there none,
Nor earth, nor water : but confusion strange ;
Mountainous ribs and adamantine limbs
Of bursten worlds, and brazen pinions vast
Of planets ship-wrecked ; many a wrinkled sun

Ate to the core by worms, with lightnings crushed;
And drossy bolts, melting like noonday snow.
Old towers of heaven were there, and fragments
      bright
Of the cerulean battlements, o'erthrown
When the gods struggled for the throne of light;
And 'mid them all a living mystery,
A shapeless image, or a vision wrapt
In clouds, and guessed at by its fearful shade;
Most like a ghost of the eternal flame,
An indistinct and unembodied horror
Which prophecies have told of; not wan Death,
Nor War the bacchanal of blood, nor Plague
The purple beast, but their great serpent-sire,
Destruction's patriarch, (dread name to speak!)
The End of all, the Universe's Death.
At that dread, ghostly thing, the atmosphere
And light of this, the world's, black charnel house,
Low bowed the Archimage, and thrice his life
Upraised its wing for passage; but the spell
Prevailed, and to his purposed task he rose.
He called unto the dead, and the swart powers,
That wander unconfined beyond the sight
Or thought of mortals; and, from the abyss
Of cavernous deep night, came forth the hands,
That dealt the mallet when this world of ours
Lay quivering on the anvil in its ore,—
Hands of eternal stone, which would unmesh
And fray this starry company of orbs,
As a young infant, on a dewy morn,
Rends into nought the tear-hung gossamer.
—To work they went, magician, hands, and Co,
With tongs and trowels, needles, scissors, paste,

Solder and glue, to make another world :
And, as a tinker, 'neath a highway hedge,
Turns, taps, and batters, rattles, bangs, and scrapes
A stew-pan ruinous,—or as, again,
The sibylline dame Gurton, ere she lost
Th' immortal bodkin, staunched the gaping wound
In Hodge's small-clothes famed,—so those great
          hands
Whisked round their monstrous loom, here stitch-
          ing in
An island of green vallies, fitting there
A mountain extra with a hook and eye,
Caulking the sea, hemming the continents,
And lacing all behind to keep it tight.
'Tis done,—'tis finished ; and between the thumb
Depends, and the forefinger,—like a toy,
Button with pin impaled, in winter games
That dances on the board,—and now it flies
Into the abyssal blueness, spinning and bright,
Just at old Saturn's tail.   The necromancer
Puffed from his pipe a British climate round,
And stars and moon, and angels beamed upon it.
Just as it joined the midnight choir of worlds,
It chanced a bearded sage espied its sweep,
And named it GEORGIUM SIDUS.   Centuries
Danc'd o'er it, but . . . . .

## THE ROMANCE OF THE LILY.

EVER love the lily pale,
The flower of ladies' breasts ;

For there is passion on its cheek,
 Its leaves a timorous sorrow speak,
And its perfume sighs a gentle tale
To its own young buds, and the wooing gale,
 And the piteous dew that near it rests.
It is no earthly common flower
 For man to pull, and maidens wear
 On the wreathed midnight of their hair.
Deep affection is its dower ;
 For Venus kissed it as it sprung,
 And gave it one immortal tear,
 When the forgotten goddess hung,
 Woe-bowed o'er Adon's daisied bier :
Its petals, brimmed with cool sweet air,
Are chaste as the words of a virgin's prayer ;
 And it lives alight in the greenwood shade,
 Like a love-thought, chequered o'er with fear,
In the memory of that self-same maid.

I ever have loved the lily pale,
 For the sake of one whom heaven has ta'en
 From the prison of man, the palace of pain.
 In autumn, Mary, thou didst die ;
(Die ! no, thou didst not—but some other way
Wentest to bliss ; she could not die like men ;
 Immortal into immortality
She went ; our sorrows know she went :) and then
 We laid her in a grassy bed
 (The mortal her) to live for ever,
 And there was nought above her head,
 No flower to bend, no leaf to quiver.
At length, in spring, her beauty dear,
Awakened by my well-known tear,

And at its thrill returning,
  Or her love and anguish burning,
    Wrought spells within the earth ;
    For a human bloom, a baby flower,
  Uprose in talismanic birth ;
Where foliage was forbid to wave,
    Engendered by no seed or shower,
A lily grew on Mary's grave.

Last eve I lay by that blossom fair,
  Alone I lay to think and weep ;
An awe was on the fading hour :
And 'midst the sweetness of the flower
There played a star of plumage rare,
  A bird from off the ebon trees,
    That grow o'er midnight's rocky steep ;
One of those whose glorious eyes,
  In myriads sown, the restless sees,
And thinks what lustrous dew there lies
Upon the violets of the skies :—
  And to itself unnumbered ditties
    Sang that angel nightingale,
  Secrets of the heavenly cities ;
    And many a strange and fearful word,
    ·Which in her arbour she had heard,
    When the court of seraphs sate
    To seal some ghost's eternal fate ;
And the wind, beneath whose current deep
My soul was pillowed in her sleep,
    Thus breathed the mystic warbler's tale.—

KING BALTHASAR has a tower of gold,
  And rubies pave his hall ;

A magic sun of diamond blazes
　　Above his palace wall ;.
And beaming spheres play round in mazes,
With locks of incense o'er them rolled.
　　　Young Balthasar is the Libyan king,
　　The lord of wizard sages ;
　　　He hath read the sun, he hath read the moon,—
Heaven's thoughts are on their pages ;
　　　He knows the meaning of night and noon,
　　　And the spell on morning's wing :
The ocean he hath studied well,
　　Its maddest waves he hath subdued
　　　Beneath an icy yoke,
　　　And lashed them till they howled, and spoke
　　The mysteries of the Titan brood,
And all their god forbade them tell.
　　He hath beheld the storm,
　·　When the phantom of its form
　　　Leans out of heaven to trace,
　　　　Upon the earth and sea,
　　　And air's cerulean face,
In earthquake, thunder, war, and fire,
And pestilence, and madness dire,
　　　That mighty woe, futurity.

From the roof of his tower he talks to Jove,
As the god enthroned sits above :
Night roosts upon his turret's height,
And the sun is the clasp of its girdle of light ;
And the stars upon his terrace dwell :—
But the roots of that tower are snakes in hell.
Balthasar's soul is a curse and a sin,
And nothing is human that dwells within,

But a tender, beauteous love,
　　That grows upon his haunted heart,
Like a scented bloom on a madhouse-wall;
For, amid the wrath and roar of all,
　　It gathers life with blessed art,
And calmly blossoms on above.

Bright Sabra, when thy thoughts are seen
　　Moving within those azure eyes,
Like spirits in a star at e'en;
　　And when that little dimple flies,
　　　As air upon a rosy bush,
　　　To hide behind thy fluttering blush;
When kisses those rich lips unclose,
And love's own music from them flows;
A god might love,—a demon does.
—'Tis night upon the sprinkled sky,
And on their couch of roses
　　The king and lady lie,
　　While the tremulous lid of each discloses
　　　A narrow streak of the living eye;
As when a beetle, afloat in the sun,
On a rocking leaf, has just begun
　　To sever the clasp of his outer wing,
　　　So lightly, that you scarce can see
His little, lace pinions' delicate fold,
And a line of his body of breathing gold,
　　Girt with many a panting ring,
Before it quivers, and shuts again,
Like a smothered regret in the breast of men,
　　Or a sigh on the lips of chastity.

One bright hand, dawning through her hair,
Bids it be black, itself as fair

As the cold moon's palest daughter,
The last dim star, with doubtful ray
Snow-like melting into day,
  Echoed to the eye on water :
Round his neck and on his breast
  The other curls, and bends its bell
  Petalled inward as it fell,
Like a tented flower at rest.
  She dreams of him, for rayed joys hover
    In dimples round her timorous lip,
  And she turns to clasp her sleeping lover,
Kissing the lid of his tender eye,
And brushing off the dews that lie
  Upon its lash's tip ;
And now she stirs no more,—
  But the thoughts of her breast are still,
  As a song of a frozen rill
Which winter spreads his dark roof o'er.
  In the still and moony hour
    Of that calm entwining sleep,
From the utmost tombs of earth
The vision-land of death and birth,
  Came a black, malignant power,
  A spectre of the desert deep :
And it is Plague, the spotted fiend, the drunkard
    of the tomb ;
Upon her mildewed temples the thunderbolts of
    doom,
And blight-buds of hell's red fire, like gory wounds
    in bloom,
  Are twisted for a wreath ;
And there's a chalice in her hand, whence bloody
    flashes gleam,

While struggling snakes with arrowy tongues twist
    o'er it for a steam,
And its liquor is of Phlegethon, and Ætna's wrath-
    ful stream,
    And icy dews of death.

Like a rapid dream she came,
And vanished like the flame
    Of a burning ship at sea,
But to his shrinking lips she pressed
    The cup of boiling misery,
And he quaffed it in his tortured rest,
    And woke in the pangs of lunacy.
    As a buried soul awaking
      From the cycle of its sleep,
Panic-struck and sad doth lie
Beneath its mind's dim canopy,
    And marks the stars of memory breaking
      From 'neath oblivion's ebbing deep,
While clouds of doubt bewilder the true sky,—
    So in the hieroglyphic portal
      Of his dreams sate Balthasar,
Awake amidst his slumbering senses,
    And felt as feels man's ghost immortal,
Whom the corpse's earthen fences
      From his vast existence bar.
The pestilence was in his breast,
    And boiled and bubbled o'er his brain ;
His thoughtless eyes in their unrest
    Would have burst their circling chain,
Scattering their fiery venom wide,
    But for the soft, endearing rain,
With which the trembler at his side

Fed those gushing orbs of white,
As evening feeds the waves, with looks of quiet light.
    The tear upon his cheek's fierce flush ;
  The cool breath on his brow ;
    And the healthy presage of a blush,
      Sketched in faint tints behind his skin ;
      And the hush of settling thoughts within,
Sabra hath given, and she will need them now.
    For, as the echo of a grove,
    Keeps its dim shadow 'neath some song of love,
      And gives her life away to it in sound,
  Soft spreading her wild harmony,
  Like a tress of smoking censery,
    Or a ring of water round,—
So all the flowery wealth
Of her happiness and health
Untwined from Sabra's strength, and grew
  Into the blasted stem of Balthasar's pale life,
And his is the beauty and bliss that flew
  On the wings of her love from his sinking wife.
    The fading wanness of despair
      Was the one colour of her cheek,
    And tears upon her bosom fair
      Wrote the woe she dared not speak ;
  But life was in her.   Yes : it played
      In tremulous and fitful grace,
  Like a flame's reflected breath
  Shivering in the throes of death
    Against the monumental face
  Of some sad, voiceless marble maid.
  And what is a woman to Balthasar,
    Whom love has weakened, bowed, and
      broken ?

Upon his forehead's darksome war,
  His lip's curled meaning, yet unspoken,
The lowering of his wrinkled brow,
'Tis graved,—he spurns, he loaths her now.

Along the sea, at night's black noon,
  Alone the king and lady float,
  With music in a snowy boat,
That glides in light, an ocean-moon;
  From billow to billow it dances,
  And the spray around it glances,
  And the mimic rocks and caves,
  Beneath the mountains of the waves,
Reflect a joyous song
As the merry bark is borne along;
And now it stays its eager sail
Within a dark sepulchral vale,
  Amid the living Alps of Ocean,
'Round which the crags in tumult rise
And make a fragment of the skies;
  Beneath whose precipice's motion
The folded dragons of the deep
Lie with lidless eyes asleep:
  It pauses; and—Is that a shriek
    That agonizes the still air,
  And makes the dead day move and speak
From beneath its midnight pall,—
Or the ruined billow's fall?
    The boat is soaring lighter there,
The voice of woman sounds no more.—
That night the water-crescent bore
Dark Balthazar alone unto the living shore.

  Tears, tears for Sabra; who will weep?

O blossoms, ye have dew,
And grief-dissembling storms might strew
   Thick-dropping woe upon her sleep.
  False sea, why dost thou look like sorrow,
   Why is thy cold heart of water?
Or rather why are tears of thee
Compassionless, bad sea?
  For not a drop does thy stern spirit borrow,
   To mourn o'er beauty's fairest daughter.
  Heaven, blue heaven, thou art not kind,
   Or else the sun is not thine eye,
  For thou should'st be with weeping blind,
   Not thus forgetful, bright, and dry.
    O that I were a plume of snow,
To melt away and die
In a long chain of bubbling harmony!—
  My tribute shall be sweet tho' small;
  A cup of the vale-lily bloom
    Filled with white and liquid woe—
  Give it to her ocean-pall:
    With such deluge-seeds I'll sow
Her mighty, elemental tomb,
Until the lamentations grow
Into a foaming crop of populous overflow.


  Hither, like a bird of prey,
   Whom red anticipations feed,
  Flaming along the fearful day
   Revenge's thirsty hour doth fly.
Heaven has said a fearful word;
(Which hell's eternal labyrinths heard,
And the wave of time
Shall answer to the depths sublime,

I.                          C

Reflecting it in deed ;)
    " Balthasar the king must die."
Must die ; for all his power is fled,
    His spells dissolved, his spirits gone,
And magic cannot ease the bed
    Where lies the necromant alone.
    What thought is gnawing in his heart,
What struggles madly in his brain ?
See, the force, the fiery pain
    Of silence makes his eyeballs start.
    O ease thy bosom, dare to tell—
But grey-haired pity speaks in vain ;
    That bitter shriek, that hopeless yell,
    Has given the secret safe to hell.
Like a ruffled nightingale,
    Balanced upon dewy wings,
Through the palace weeps the tale,
    Leaving tears, where'er she sings :
And, around the icy dead,
    Maids are winding
Kingly robes of mocking lead,
    And with leafy garlands binding
The unresisting, careless head :
Gems are flashing, garments wave
'Round the bridegroom of the grave.
Hark ! A shout of wild surprise,
    A burst of terrible amaze !
The lids are moving up his eyes,
    They open, kindle, beam, and gaze.—
Grave, thy bars are broken,
    Quenched the flames of pain,
Falsely fate hath spoken,
    The dead is born again.

As when the moon and shadows' strife,
   On some rebellious night,
Looks a pale statue into life,
    And gives his watching form the action of
       their light,—
So stilly strode the awakened one,
And with the voice of stone,
  Which troubled caverns screech,
    Cursing the tempest's maniac might,
  He uttered human speech.
" Tremble, living ones, and hear ;
By the name of death and fear,
By lightning, earthquake, fire and war,
And him whose snakes and hounds they are,
From whose judgment-seat I come,
Listen, crouch, be dumb.
My soul is drowned beneath a flood
Of conscience, red with Sabra's blood ;
  And, from yon blue infinity,
    Doomed and tortured I am sent
  To confess the deed and fly :
    Wail not for me,—yourselves repent :
    Eternity is punishment ;
  Listen, crouch, and die."
    With that word his body fell,
As dust upon the storm,—
Flash-like darkened was his form ;
While through their souls in horror rang
The dragon-shout, the thunderous clang
    Of the closing gates of hell.

# PYGMALION,

## OR THE CYPRIAN STATUARY.

THERE stood a city along Cyprus' side
Lavish of palaces, an arched tide
Of unrolled rocks ; and, where the deities dwelled,
Their clustered domes pushed up the noon, and
     swelled
With the emotion of the god within,—
As doth earth's hemisphere, when showers begin
To tickle the still spirit at its core,
Till pastures tremble and the river-shore
Squeezes out buds at every dewy pore.
And there were pillars, from some mountain's heart,
Thronging beneath a wide, imperial floor
That bent with riches ; and there stood apart
A palace, oft accompanied by trees,
That laid their shadows in the galleries
Under the coming of the endless light,
Net-like ;—who trod the marble, night or day,
By moon, or lamp, or sunless day-shine white,
Would brush the shaking, ghostly leaves away,
Which might be tendrils or a knot of wine,
Burst from the depth of a faint window-vine,'
With a bird pecking it : and round the hall
And wandering staircase, within every wall
Of sea-ward portico, and sleeping chamber,
Whose patient lamp distilled a day of amber,
There stood, and sate, or made rough steeds their
     throne,

Immortal generations wrung from stone,
Alike too beautiful for life and death,
And bodies that a soul of mortal breath
Would be the dross of.

            Such a house as this     30
Within a garden hard by Salamis,
(Cyprus's city-crown and capital
Ere Paphos was, and at whose ocean-wall
Beauty and love's paternal waves do beat
That sprouted Venus ;) such a fair retreat    35
Lonely Pygmalion's self inhabited,
Whose fiery chisel with creation fed
The ship-wrecked rocks ; who paid the heavens
      again
Diamonds for ice ; who made gods who make men. / 40
Lonely Pygmalion : you might see him go
Along the streets where markets thickest flow,
Doubling his gown across his thinking breast,
And the men fall aside ; nor only pressed
Out of his elbows' way, but left a place,      45
A sun-room for him, that his mind had space
And none went near ; none in his sweep would
      venture,
For you might feel that he was but the centre
Of an inspired round, the middle spark
Of a great moon, setting aside the dark      50
And cloudy people.  As he went along
The chambered ladies silenced the half-song,
And let the wheel unheeded whirl and skim,
To get their eyes blest by the sight of him.
So locks were swept from every eye that drew    55
Sun for the soul through circles violet-blue,
Mild brown, or passionate black.

Still, discontent,
Over his sensual kind the sculptor went,
Walking his thoughts.   Yet Cyprus' girls be fair ; 60
Day-bright and evening-soft the maidens are,
And witching like the midnight, and their pleasure
Silent and deep as midnight's starry treasure.
Lovely and young, Pygmalion yet loved none.
His soul was bright and lovely as the sun,            65
Like which he could create ; and in its might
There lived another Spirit wild and bright,
That came and went ; and, when it came, its light
On these dim earthy things, turn where he will,
Its light, shape, beauty were reflected still.            70
Day-time and dark it came ; like a dim mist
Shelt'ring a god, it rolled, and, ere he wist,
It fell aside, and dawned a shape of grace,
And an inspired and melancholy face,
Whose lips were smile-buds dewy :—into him            75
It rolled like sun-light till his sight was dim,            .
And it was in his heart and soul again,
Not seen but breathed.
There was a grassy plain,
A pasture of the deer,—Olympus' mountain            80
Was the plain's night, the picture of its fountain :
Unto which unfrequented dell and wood
Unwittingly his solitary mood
Oft drew him.—In the water lay
A fragment of pale marble, which they say            85
Slipped from some fissure in the agued moon,
Which had caught earth-quake and a deadly swoon
When the sun touched her with his hilly shade.
Weeds grew upon it, and the streamlet made
A wanton music with its ragged side,            90

And birds had nests there.   One still even-tide,
When they were perched and sleeping, passed this
    man,
Startling the air with thoughts which over-ran
The compass of his mind : writing the sand
Idly he paused, and laid unwitting hand                 95
On the cold stone.   How smooth the touch !   It
    felt
Less porous than a lip which kisses melt,
And  diamond-hard.    That  night  his  workmen
    wrought
With iron under it, and it was brought,
This dripping quarry, while the sky was starry,        100
Home to the weary, yearning statuary.
He saw no sky that day, no dark that night,
For through the hours his lamp was full of light,
Shadowing the pavement with his busy right.
Day after day they saw not in the street                105
The wondrous artist : some immortal feat
Absorbed him ; and yet often in the noon,
When the town slept beneath the sweltering June,
—The rich within, the poor man on the stair,—
He stole unseen into the meadow's air,                  110
And fed on sight of summer, till the life
Was too abundant in him ; and so, rife
With light creative, he went in alone,
And poured it warm upon the growing stone.
The magic chisel thrust, and gashed, and swept,        115
Flying and manifold ; no cloud e'er wept
So fast, so thick, so light upon the close
Of shapeless green it meant to make a rose :—
And as insensibly out of a stick,
Dead in the winter-time, the dew-drops quick,          120

And the thin sun-beams, and the airy shower
Raise and unwrap a many-leaved flower,
And then a fruit: so from the barren stock
Of the deer-shading, formless valley-rock,
This close stone-bud, he, quiet as the air,      125
Had shaped a lady wonderfully fair,
—Dear to the eyes, a delicate delight,—
For all her marble symmetry was white
As brow and bosom should be, save some azure
Which waited for a loving lip's erasure,      130
Upon her shoulder, to be turned to blush.
And she was smooth and full, as if one gush
Of life had washed her, or as if a sleep
Lay on her eye-lid, easier to sweep
Than bee from daisy.   Who could help a sigh      135
At seeing a beauty stand so lifelessly,
But that it was too beautiful to die?
Dealer of immortality,
Greater than Jove himself,—for only he
Can such eternize as the grave has ta'en,      140
And open heaven by the gate of pain,—
What art thou now, divine Pygmalion?
Divine! gods counting human.   Thou hast done
That glory, which has undone thee for ever.
For thou art weak, and tearful, and dost shiver      145
Wintrily sad; and thy life's healthy river,
With which thy body once was overflown,
Is dried and sunken to its banks of bone.
He carved it not; nor was the chisel's play,
That dashed the earthen hindrances away,      150
Driven and diverted by his muscle's sway.
The winged tool, as digging out a spell,
Followed a magnet wheresoe'er it fell,

That sucked and led it right : and for the rest,
The living form, with which the stone he blest,          155
Was the loved image stepping from his breast.
And therefore loves he it, and therefore stays
About the she-rock's feet, from hour to hour,
Anchored to her by his own heart : the power
Of the isle's Venus therefore thus he prays.          160
"Goddess, that made me, save thy son, and save
The man, that made thee goddess, from the grave.
Thou know'st it not ; it is a fearful coop,—
Dark, cold, and horrible,—a blinded loop
In Pluto's madhouse' green and wormy wall.          165
O save me from't ! Let me not die, like all ;
For I am but like one : not yet, not yet,
At least not yet ; and why ? My eyes are wet
With the thick dregs of immature despair ;
With bitter blood out of my empty heart.          170
I breathe not aught but my own sighs for air,
And my life's strongest is a dying start.
No sour grief there is to me unwed ;
I could not be more lifeless being dead.
Then let me die. . Ha ! did she pity me ?          175
Oh ! she can never love. Did you not see,
How still she bears the music of my moan !
Her heart? Ah ! touch it. Fool ! I love the stone.
Inspire her, gods ! oft ye have wasted life
On the deformed, the hideous, and the vile :          180
Oh ! grant it my sweet rock,—my only wife.
I do not ask it long : a little while,—
A year,—a day,—an hour,—let it be !
For that I'll give you my eternity.
Or let it be a fiend, if ye will send          185
Something, yon form to humanize and bend,

Within those limbs,—and, when the new-poured
    blood
Flows in such veins, the worst must turn to good.
They will not hear. Thou, Jove,—or thou,
    Apollo—
Ay, thou ! thou know'st,—O listen to my groan. 190
'Twas Niobe thou drov'st from flesh to stone :
Shew this the hole she broke, and let her follow
That mother's track of steps and eyelid rain,
Treading them backwards into life again.
Life, said I ? Lives she not ? Is there not gone 195
My life into her, which I pasture on ;
Dead, where she is not ? Live, thou statue fair,
Live, thou dear marble,—or I shall go wild.
I cover thee, my sweet ; I leave thee there,
Behind this curtain, my delicious child, 200
That they may secretly begin to give
My prayer to thee : when I return, O live !
Oh ! live,—or I live not." And so he went,
Leaving the statue in its darksome tent.
    Morn after morn, sadder the artist came ; 205
His prayer, his disappointment were the same.
But when he gazed she was more near to woman ;
There was a fleshy pink, a dimple wrought
That trembled, and the cheek was growing human
With the flushed distance of a rising thought, 210
That still crept nearer :—yet no further sign !
And now, Pygmalion, that weak life of thine
Shakes like a dew-drop in a broken rose,
Or incense parting from the altar-glows.
'Tis the last look,—and he is mad no more : 215
By rule and figure he could prove at large
She never can be born,—and from the shore

His foot is stretching into Charon's barge.
Upon the pavement ghastly is he lying,
Cold with the last and stoniest embrace :  220
Elysium's light illumines all his face ;
His eyes have a wild, starry grace
Of heaven, into whose depth of depths he's dying.
—A sound, with which the air doth shake,
Extinguishing the window of moonlight !  225
A pang of music dropping round delight,
As if sweet music's honiest heart did break !
Such a flash, and such a sound, the world
Is stung by, as if something was unfurled
That held great bliss within its inmost curled.  230
Roof after roof, the palace rends asunder ;
And then—O sight of joy and placid wonder !
He lies, beside a fountain, on the knee
Of the sweet woman-statue, quietly
Weeping the tears of his felicity.  235

# LINES

### WRITTEN IN A BLANK LEAF OF THE 'PROMETHEUS UNBOUND.'

WRITE it in gold—A spirit of the sun,
An intellect a-blaze with heavenly thoughts,
A soul with all the dews of pathos shining,
Odorous with love, and sweet to silent woe
With the dark glories of concentrate song,
Was sphered in mortal earth.  Angelic sounds
Alive with panting thoughts sunned the dim world.

The bright creations of an human heart
Wrought magic in the bosoms of mankind.
A flooding summer burst on poetry;
Of which the crowning sun, the night of beauty,
The dancing showers, the birds, whose anthems
     wild
Note after note unbind the enchanted leaves
Of breaking buds, eve, and the flow of dawn,
Were centred and condensed in his one name
As in a providence,—and that was SHELLEY.

*Oxford*, 1822.


## SONNET :

### TO TARTAR, A TERRIER BEAUTY.

SNOW-DROP of dogs, with ear of brownest dye,
Like the last orphan leaf of naked tree
Which shudders in bleak autumn; though by thee,
Of hearing careless and untutored eyes,
Not understood articulate speech of men,
Nor marked the artificial mind of books,
—The mortal's voice eternized by the pen,—
Yet hast thou thought and language all unknown
To Babel's scholars; oft intensest looks,
Long scrutiny o'er some dark-veined stone
Dost thou bestow, learning dead mysteries
Of the world's birth-day, oft in eager tone
With quick-tailed fellows bandiest prompt replies,
Solicitudes canine, four-footed amities.

# LETTER TO B. W. PROCTER, ESQ.

## FROM OXFORD; MAY, 1825.

In every tower, that Oxford has, is swung,
Quick, loud, or solemn, the monotonous tongue
Which speaks Time's language, the universal one
After the countenance of 'moon or sun,—
Translating their still motions to the earth.
I cannot read ; the reeling belfry's mirth
Troubles my senses ; therefore, Greek, shut up
Your dazzling pages ; covered be the cup
Which Homer has beneath his mantle old,
Steamy with boiling life : your petals fold
You fat, square blossoms of the yet young tree
Of Britain-grafted, flourishing Germany :
Hush ! Latin, to your grave :—and, with the
      chime,
My pen shall turn the minutes into rhyme,
And, like the dial, blacken them.   There sits,
Or stands, or lounges, or perhaps on bits
Of this rag's daughter, paper, exorcises,
With strange black marks and inky wild devices,
The witch of worlds, the echo of great verse,
About the chasms of the universe,
Ringing and bounding immortality.—
Give him thy bosom, dark Melpomene,
And let him of thy goblet and thine eye
Exhaust the swimming, deep insanity.
He hath the soul, O let it then be fed,
Sea after sea, with that which is not read,

Nor wrung by reasoning from a resolute head,
But comes like lightning on a hill-top steeple ;
Heaven's spillings on the lofty laurelled people.
Verse to thee, light to thee, wings upraise thee
          long
In the unvacillating soar of song,
Thou star-seed of a man !  But do not dare
To tempt thy Apollonian god too far,
Clogging and smoking thy young snake, Renown,
In the strait, stony shadows of the town,
Lest he grow weak, and pine, and never be
What he was born, twin to Eternity.
So come, shake London from thy skirts away :
So come, forget not it is England's May.
For Oxford, ho ! by moonlight or by sun :
Our horses are not hours, but rather run
Foot by foot faster than the second-sand,
While the old sunteam, like a plough, doth stand
Stuck in thick heaven.   Here thou at morn shalt
          see
Spring's dryad-wakening whisper call the tree,
And move it to green answers ; and beneath,
Each side the river which the fishes breathe,
Daisies and grass, whose tops were never stirred,
Or dews made tremulous, but by foot of bird.
And you shall mark in spring's heaven-tapestried
          room
Yesterday's knoppe, burst by its wild perfume,
Like woman's childhood, to this morning's bloom ;
And here a primrose pale beneath a tree,
And here a cowslip longing for its bee,
And violets and lilies every one
Grazing in the great pasture of the sun,

Beam after beam, visibly as the grass
Is swallowed by the lazy cows that pass.
Come look, come walk,—and there shall suddenly
Seize you a rapture and a phantasy ;
High over mountain sweeping, fast and high
Through all the intricacies of the sky,
As fast and far a ship-wrecked hoard of gold
Dives ocean, cutting every billow's fold.
These are the honey-minutes of the year
Which make man god, and make a god—Shake-
      speare.
Come, gather them with me. . If not, then go,
And with thee all the ghosts of Jonson's toe,
The fighting Tartars and the Carthaginians :
And may your lady-muse's stiff-winged pinions
Be naked and impossible to fly,
Like a fat goose pen-plucked for poetry.
A curse upon thy cream to make it sour :
A curse upon thy tea-pot every hour ;
Spirits of ice possess it ! and thy tea,
Changed at its contact, hay and straw leaves be !
A cold and nipping ague on thine urn !
And an invisible canker eat and burn
The mathematic picture, near your fire,
Of the grave, compass-handed, quiet sire !
No more.—Be these the visions of your sorrow
When you have read this doggrel through to-
      morrow,
And then refuse to let our Oxford borrow
You of the smoky-faced, Augustan town,
And unpersuaded drop the paper down.

# ANOTHER LETTER TO THE SAME.

## FROM GÖTTINGEN; MARCH 13, 1836.

To-day a truant from the odd, old bones
And winds of flesh, which, as tamed rocks and
    stones
Piled cavernously make his body's dwelling,
Have housed man's soul : there, where time's
    billows swelling
Make a deep, ghostly, and invisible sea
Of melted worlds antediluvially,
Upon the sand of ever-crumbling hours,
God-founded, stands the castle, all its towers
With veiny tendrils ivied :—this bright day ·
I leave its chambers, and with oars away
Seek some enchanted island, where to play.
And what do you that in the enchantment dwell,
And should be raving ever ? a wild swell
Of passionate life rolling about the world,
Now sun-sucked to the clouds, dashed on the
    curled
Leaf-hidden daisies, an incarnate storm
Letting the sun through on the meadows yellow,
Or anything except that earthy fellow,
That wise dog's brother, man.  O shame to tell !
Make tea in Circe's cup, boil the cool well,
The well Pierian,.which no bird dare sip
But nightingales.  There let kettles dip
Who write their simpering sonnets to its song,
And walk on Sundays in Parnassus' park :—

Take thy example from the sunny lark,
Throw off the mantle which conceals the soul,
The many-citied world, and seek thy goal
Straight as a star-beam falls. · Creep not nor climb,
As they who place their topmost of sublime
On some peak of this planet, pitifully.
Dart eagle-wise with open wings, and fly
Until you meet the gods.   Thus counsel I
The men who can, but tremble to be, great:
Cursed be the fool who taught to hesitate,
And to regret : time lost most bitterly !
And thus I write, and I dare write, to thee,
Fearing that still, as you were wont to do,
You feed and fear some asinine review.
Let Juggernaut roll on ; and we, whose sires
Blooded his wheels and prayed around his fires,
Laugh at the leaden ass in the god's skin.
Example follows precept.   I have been
Giving some negro minutes of the night,
Freed from the slavery of my ruling spright
Anatomy the grim, to a new story,
In whose satiric pathos we will glory.
In it Despair has married wildest Mirth,
And, to their wedding-banquet, all the earth
Is bade to bring its enmities and loves,
Triumphs and horrors : you shall see the doves
Billing with quiet joy, and all the while
Their nest's the scull of some old king of Nile.
But he who fills the cups, and makes the jest,
Pipes to the dancers, is the fool o' th' feast,—
Who's he? .I've dug him up and decked him trim,
And made a mock, a fool, a slave of him,
Who was the planet's tyrant, dotard Death ;

I.                                                    D

Man's hate and dread.　Not, with a stoical breath,
To meet him, like Augustus, standing up ;
Nor with grave saws to season the cold cup,
Like the philosopher; nor yet to hail
His coming with a verse or jesting tale,
As Adrian did and More :—but of his night,
His moony ghostliness, and silent might
To rob him, to uncypress him i' the light,
To unmask all his secrets ; make him play
Momus o'er wine by torch-light,—is the way
To conquer him, and kill ; and from the day,
Spurn'd, hiss'd, and hooted, send him back again,
An unmask'd braggart to his bankrupt den.
For death is more "a jest" than life : you see
Contempt grows quick from familiarity.
I owe this wisdom to Anatomy.—
Your Muse is younger in her soul than mine :
O feed her still on woman's smiles and wine,
And give the world a tender song once more ;
For all the good can love and can adore
What's human, fair, and gentle.　Few, I know,
Can bear to sit at my board, when I show
The wretchedness and folly of man's all,
And laugh myself right heartily.　Your call
Is higher and more human : I will do
Unsociably my part, and still be true
To my own soul ; but e'er admire you,
And own that you have nature's kindest trust,
Her weak and dear to nourish,—that I must.
Then fare, as you deserve it, well, and live
In the calm feelings you to others give.

# THE BODING DREAMS.

## I.

In lover's ear a wild voice cried :
  "Sleeper, awake and rise !"
A pale form stood by his bed-side,
  With heavy tears in her sad eyes.
"A beckoning hand, a moaning sound,
A new-dug grave in weedy ground
For her who sleeps in dreams of thee.
Awake !  Let not the murder be !"
Unheard the faithful dream did pray,
And sadly sighed itself away.
  "Sleep on," sung Sleep, "to-morrow
  'Tis time to know thy sorrow."
  "Sleep on," sung Death, "to-morrow
  From me thy sleep thou'lt borrow."
    Sleep on, lover, sleep on,
      The tedious dream is gone ;
        The bell tolls one.

## II.

Another hour, another dream :
  "Awake ! awake !" it wailed,
"Arise, ere with the moon's last beam
  Her rosy life hath paled."
A hidden light, a muffled tread,
A daggered hand beside the bed
Of her who sleeps in dreams of thee.
Thou wak'st not : let the murder be.

In vain the faithful dream did pray,
And sadly sighed itself away.
  " Sleep on," sung Sleep, " to-morrow
  'Tis time to know thy sorrow."
  " Sleep on," sung Death, " to-morrow
  From me thy sleep thou'lt borrow."
      Sleep on, lover, sleep on,
      The tedious dream is gone ;
        Soon comes the sun.


### III.

Another hour, another dream :
  A red wound on a snowy breast,
A rude hand stifling the last scream,
  On rosy lips a death-kiss pressed.
Blood on the sheets, blood on the floor,
The murderer stealing through the door.
" Now," said the voice, with comfort deep,
" She sleeps indeed, and thou may'st sleep."
The scornful dream then turned away
To the first, bleeding cloud of day.
  " Sleep on," sung Sleep, " to-morrow
  'Tis time to know thy sorrow."
  " Sleep on," sung Death, " to-morrow
  From me thy sleep thou'lt borrow."
      Sleep on, lover, sleep on,
      The tedious dream is gone ;
        The murder's done.

## SONG OF A MAID WHOSE LOVE IS DEAD.

MERRY, merry little stream,
  Tell me, hast thou seen my dear?
I left him with an azure dream,
  Calmly sleeping on his bier—
    But he has fled !

" I passed him in his church-yard bed—
A yew is sighing o'er his head,
And grass-roots mingle with his hair."
  What doth he there?
O cruel! can he lie alone?
  Or in the arms of one more dear?
Or hides he in that bower of stone,
  To cause and kiss away my fear?.

" He doth not speak, he doth not moan—
Blind, motionless he lies alone ;
But, ere the grave snake fleshed his sting,
This one warm tear he bade me bring
  And lay it at thy feet
  Among the daisies sweet."

Moonlight whisperer, summer air,
  Songster of the groves above,
Tell the maiden rose I wear,
  Whether thou hast seen my love.
" This night in heaven I saw him lie,
  Discontented with his bliss ;
  And on my lips he left this kiss,
For thee to taste and then to die." ...

# THE GHOSTS' MOONSHINE.

### I.

IT is midnight, my wedded ;
  Let us lie under
The tempest bright undreaded,
  In the warm thunder :
(Tremble and weep not !  What can you fear ?)
  My heart's best wish is thine,—
That thou wert white, and bedded
  On the softest bier,
    In the ghosts' moonshine.
  Is that the wind ?  No, no ;
  Only two devils, that blow
  Through the murderer's ribs to and fro,
    In the ghosts' moonshine.

### II.

Who is there, she said afraid, yet
  Stirring and awaking
The poor old dead ?  His spade, it
  Is only making,—
(Tremble and weep not !  What do you crave ?)
  Where yonder grasses twine,
A pleasant bed, my maid, that
  Children call a grave,
    In the cold moonshine.
  Is that the wind ?  No, no ;
  Only two devils, that blow
  Through the murderer's ribs to and fro,
    In the ghosts' moonshine.

### III.

What dost thou strain above her
 Lovely throat's whiteness?
A silken chain, to cover
 Her bosom's brightness?
(Tremble and weep not: what dost thou fear?)
 —My blood is spilt like wine,
Thou hast strangled and slain me, lover,
 Thou hast stabbed me dear,
 In the ghosts' moonshine.
 Is that the wind? No, no;
 Only her goblin doth blow
 Through the murderer's ribs to and fro,
 In its own moonshine.


## FROM THE GERMAN.

### I.

" COME with me, thou gentle maid,
The stars are strong, and make a shade
Of yew across your mother's tomb;
Leave your chamber's vine-leaved gloom,
 Leave your harp-strings, loved one,
'Tis our hour; " the robber said;
 " Yonder comes the goblins' sun,
For, when men are still in bed,
Day begins with the old dead.
Leave your flowers so dewed with weeping,
And our feverish baby sleeping;
Come to me, thou gentle maid,
'Tis our hour." The robber said.

### II.

To the wood, whose shade is night,
Went they in the owls' moonlight.
As they passed, the common wild
Like a murderous jester smiled,
  Dimpled twice with nettly graves.
You may mark her garment white,
  In the night-wind how it waves :
The night-wind to the churchyard flew,
And whispered underneath the yew ;
" Mother churchyard, in my breath,
I've a lady's sigh of death."
—" Sleep thou there, thou robber's wife."
Said he, clasping his wet knife.


## THE PHANTOM-WOOER.

### I.

A GHOST, that loved a lady fair,
Ever in the starry air
  Of midnight at her pillow stood ;
And, with a sweetness skies above
The luring words of human love,
  Her soul the phantom wooed.
Sweet and sweet is their poisoned note,
The little snakes' of silver throat,
In mossy skulls that nest and lie,
Ever singing " die, oh! die."

### II.

Young soul, put off your flesh, and come
With me into the quiet tomb,

Our bed is lovely, dark, and sweet ;
The earth will swing us, as she goes,
Beneath our coverlid of snows,
  And the warm leaden sheet.
Dear and dear is their poisoned note,
The little snakes' of silver throat,
In mossy skulls that nest and lie,
Ever singing "die, oh ! die."


## A DIRGE.

TO-DAY is a thought, a fear is to-morrow,
And yesterday is our sin and our sorrow ;
  And life is a death,
    Where the body's the tomb,
  And the pale sweet breath
    Is buried alive in its hideous gloom.
  Then waste no tear,
    For we are the dead ; the living are here,
  In the stealing earth, and the heavy bier.
Death lives but an instant, and is but a sigh,
And his son is unnamed immortality,
Whose being is thine.   Dear ghost, so to die
Is to live,—and life is a worthless lie.—
Then we weep for ourselves, and wish thee good-
    bye.

## ANOTHER DIRGE.

### (FOR A YOUNG MAIDEN.)

HUSHED be sighing, near the string,
O'er whose tremors deep we sing
The youngest Death, who hath no fears,
Blood, nor pang, nor any tears.
    Hushed be sighing !
Fair and young as Venus' child,
Only paler, and most mild ;
End of all that's dear and young,
    Thee we mean, soft Drop of roses ;
Hush of birds that sweetest sung,
    That beginn'st when music closes ;
    The maiden's Dying !


## BRIDAL SERENADE.

MAIDEN, thou sittest alone above,
    Crowned with flowers, and like a sprite
    Starrily clothed in a garment white :
Thou art the only maiden I love,
    And a soul of fondness to thee I bring,
    Thy glorious beauty homaging,—
    But ah ! thou wearest a golden ring.
Maiden, thou'st broken no vow to me,
    But undone me alone with gentleness,
    Wasting upon me glances that bless ;
And knew'st that I never was born for thee.
    No hope, no joy ; yet never more

My heart shall murmur; now 'tis o'er,
I'll bless thee dying at thy door.


## DIRGE.

To her couch of evening rest
'Neath the sun's divinest west,
Bear we, in the silent car,
This consumed incense star,
This dear maid whose life is shed,
And whose sweets are sweetly dead.


## DIRGE AND HYMENEAL:

### SUPPOSED TO BE SUNG AS THE FUNERAL AND WEDDING PROCESSIONS CROSS EACH OTHER AT THE CHURCH-DOOR.

*Dirge.*

WOE! woe! this is death's hour
Of spring; behold his flower!
Fair babe of life, to whom
Death, and the dreamy tomb,
Was nothing yesterday,
   And now is all!
The maiden, from her play
Beside her lover gay,
  The church-yard voices call,
    Tolling so slow,
      Woe! woe!

### *Hymeneal.*

Joy! joy! it is love's day;
Strew the young conqueror's way
With summer's glories young,
O'er which the birds have sung,
Bright weeds from fairy rings;
   Here, there, away!
Joy, joy the tree-bird sings,
Joy, joy, a hundred springs
 Melodies ever say,—
    Maiden and boy,
      Joy! joy!

### *Dirge.*

SHE cut the roses down,
And wreathed her bridal crown.
Death, playful, culled her blossom,
And tore her from life's bosom.
Fair maiden, or fair ghost,—
   Which is thy name?—
Come to the spectral host;
They pity thee the most,
   And, to the cold world's shame,
    Soft cry they, low,
      Woe! woe!

# DIAL-THOUGHTS.

### I.

I THINK of thee at day-break still,
  And then thou art my playmate small,
Beside our straw-roofed village rill
  Gathering cowslips tall,
And chasing oft the butterfly,
  Which flutters past like treacherous life.
You smile at me and at you I,
  A husband boy and baby wife.

### II.

I think of thee at noon again,
  And thy meridian beauty high
Falls on my bosom, like young rain,
  Out of a summer sky :
And I reflect it in the tear,
  Which 'neath thy picture drops forlorn,
And then my love is bright and clear,
  And manlier than it was at morn.

### III.

I think of thee by evening's star,
  And softly melancholy, slow,
An eye doth glisten from afar,
  All full of lovely woe.
The air then sighingly doth part,
  And, or from Death the cold, or Love,
I hear the passing of a dart,
  But hope once more, and look above.

IV.

I think of thee at black midnight,
  And woe and agony it is
To see thy cheek so deadly white,
  To hear thy grave-worm hiss.
But looking on thy lips is cheer,
  They closed in love, pronouncing love ;
And then I tremble, not for fear,
  But in thy breath from heaven above.

## DREAM-PEDLARY.

I.

IF there were dreams to sell,
  What would you buy?
Some cost a passing bell ;
  Some a light sigh,
That shakes from Life's fresh crown
Only a rose-leaf down.
If there were dreams to sell,
Merry and sad to tell,
And the crier rung the bell,
  What would you buy?

II.

A cottage lone and still,
  With bowers nigh,
Shadowy, my woes to still,
  Until I die.

Such pearl from Life's fresh crown
Fain would I shake me down.
Were dreams to have at will,
This would best heal my ill,
  This would I buy.


### III.

But there were dreams to sell
  Ill didst thou buy;
Life is a dream, they tell,
  Waking, to die.
Dreaming a dream to prize,
Is wishing ghosts to rise;
  And, if I had the spell
  To call the buried well,
    Which one would I?


### IV.

If there are ghosts to raise,
  What shall I call,
Out of hell's murky haze,
  Heaven's blue pall?
Raise my loved long-lost boy
To lead me to his joy.—
  There are no ghosts to raise;
  Out of death lead no ways;
    Vain is the call.


### V.

Know'st thou not ghosts to sue
  No love thou hast.
Else lie, as I will do,
  And breathe thy last.

So out of Life's fresh crown
Fall like a rose-leaf down.
　Thus are the ghosts to woo ;
　Thus are all dreams made true,
　　Ever to last !


## BALLAD OF HUMAN LIFE.

### I.

WHEN we were girl and boy together,
　We tossed about the flowers
　And wreathed the blushing hours
Into a posy green and sweet.
　I sought the youngest, best,
　And never was at rest
Till I had laid them at thy fairy feet.
But the days of childhood they were fleet,
　And the blooming sweet-briar breathed weather,
　When we were boy and girl together.

### II.

Then we were lad and lass together,
　And sought the kiss of night
　Before we felt aright,
Sitting and singing soft and sweet.
　The dearest thought of heart
　With thee 'twas joy to part,
And the greater half was thine, as meet.
Still my eyelid's dewy, my veins they beat
　At the starry summer-evening weather,
　When we were lad and lass together.

### III.

And we are man and wife together,
  Although thy breast, once bold
  With song, be closed and cold
Beneath flowers' roots and birds' light feet.
  Yet sit I by thy tomb,
  And dissipate the gloom
With songs of loving faith and sorrow sweet.
And fate and darkling grave kind dreams do cheat,
That, while fair life, young hope, despair and
      death are,
  We're boy and girl, and lass and lad, and man
    and wife together.


## SONG, ON THE WATER.

### I.

WILD with passion, sorrow-beladen,
  Bend the thought of thy stormy soul
On its home, on its heaven, the loved maiden;
  And peace shall come at her eyes' control.
Even so night's starry rest possesses
  With its gentle spirit these tamed waters,
And bids the wave, with weedy tresses
  Embower the ocean's pavement stilly
  Where the sea-girls lie, the mermaid-daughters,
    Whose eyes, not born to weep,
    More palely-lidded sleep,
  Than in our fields the lily;
    And sighing in their rest
      More sweet than is its breath;
      And quiet as its death
        Upon a lady's breast.

I.                                                    E

II.

Heart high-beating, triumph-bewreathed,
  Search the record of loves gone by,
And borrow the blessings by them bequeathed
  To deal from out of thy victory's sky.
Even so, throughout the midnight deep,
  The silent moon doth seek the bosoms
Of those dear mermaid-girls asleep,
    To feed its dying rays anew,
    Like to the bee on earthly blossoms,
      Upon their silvery whiteness,
      And on the rainbow brightness
Of their eyelashes' dew,
    And kisseth their limbs o'er :
      Her lips where they do quaff
      Strike starry tremors off,
        As from the waves our oar.

## LOVE-IN-IDLENESS.

I.

"SHALL I be your first love, lady, shall I be
    your first ?
  Oh ! then I'll fall before you, down on my velvet
    knee,
  And deeply bend my rosy head and press it upon
    thee,
And swear that there is nothing more, for which
    my heart doth thirst,
    But a downy kiss, and pink,
    Between your lips' soft chink."

## II.

"Yes, you shall be my first love, boy, and you
  shall be my first,
 And I will raise you up again unto my bosom's
  fold ;
 And, when you kisses many one on lip and
  cheek have told,
I'll let you loose upon the grass, to leave me if you
  durst ;
  And so we'll toy away
  The night besides the day."


## III.

"But let me be your second love, but let me be
  your second,
 For then I'll tap so gently, dear, upon your
  window pane,
 And creep between the curtains in, where never
  man has lain,
And never leave thy gentle side till the morning
  star hath beckoned,
  Within the silken lace
  Of thy young arms' embrace."


## IV.

"Well thou shalt be my second love, yes, gentle
  boy, my second,
 And I will wait at eve for thee within my lonely
  bower,
 And yield unto thy kisses, like a bud to April's
  shower,
From moon-set till the tower-clock the hour of
  dawn hath reckoned,

And lock thee with my arms
All silent up in charms."

### V.

" No, I will be thy third love, lady, ay I will be
the third,
And break upon thee, bathing, in woody place
alone,
And catch thee to my saddle and ride o'er stream
and stone,
And press thee well, and kiss thee well, and never
speak a word,
'Till thou hast yielded up
The margin of love's cup."

### VI.

" Then thou shalt not be my first love, boy, nor
my second, nor my third;
If thou'rt the first, I'll laugh at thee, and pierce
thy flesh with thorns;
If the second, from my chamber pelt with jeer-
ing laugh and scorns;
And if thou darest be the third, I'll draw my dirk
unheard
And cut thy heart in two,—
And then die, weeping you."


## THE REASON WHY.

### I.

I LOVE thee and I love thee not,
I love thee, yet I'd rather not,
All of thee, yet I know not what.

A flowery eye as tender,
A swan-like neck as slender,
And on it a brown little spot
   For tears to fall afraid on,
   And kisses to be paid on,
Have other maidens too.
Then why love I, love, none but you?
If I could find the reason why,
Methinks my love would quickly die.

II.

Ay, knew I how to hate thee, maid,
I'd hate thee for I knew not what,
Excepting that I'd rather not
   Be thy friend or foeman;
   For thou'rt the only woman,
   On whom to think my heart's afraid;
     For, if I would abhor thee,
     The more must I long for thee.
   What others force me to,
   I turn me from; why not from you?
If I could find the reason why,
My disenchanted love would die.

III.

But should'st thou cease my heart to move
To longings, that I'd rather not,
And tried I hate, I know not what
   My heart would do for mourning;
   Love I,—it bursts, love scorning.
   O loveliest hate, most hateful love,
     This combat and endeavour
     Is what enslaves me ever.

I'll neither of the two,
Or hate or love the love of you.
And now I've found the reason why,
I know my love can never die.


## THE TWO ARCHERS.

### I.

AT break of bright May-morning,
  When, triumphing o'er dark,
  The sun's inspired lark,
All sprites and spectres scorning,
And laughing at all creatures' joys
Who could not hang, and dive, and poise
In their own web and flood of noise,
  Dropped, out of his heart's treasure,
    The sunbeam's path along,
    Sparks and dews of song,
  As if there were no pleasure
    But to rise and sing and fly,
    Winged and all soul, into the sky :

### II.

At break of this May-morning,
  A maiden young and coy
  Saw a wild archer boy
Flying around and scorning,
Birdlike, a withered bowman's arts,
Who aimed, as he, at roses' hearts.
Each cried " Come buy my darts,
  They are with magic laden
    To deify the blood ;
    An angel in the bud,

Half-closed, is a maiden,
    Till, opened by such wound, she fly,
    Winged and all soul, into the sky."


### III.

" You archers of May-morning,"
    Said she, " if I must choose,
    Such joy is to peruse,
In the star-light adorning,
The urchin's eye, that my desire
Is for his darts, whose breath fans higher
The smitten roses like a fire."
    So Love,—'twas he,—shot smiling
        His shaft, then flew away;
        Alas ! that morn of May !
    Love fled, there's no beguiling
        Repentance, but by hopes to fly,
        Winged and all soul, into the sky.


### IV.

So one December morning,
    When the bold lark no more
    Rebuked the ghosts so sore,
When dews were not adorning
Ought but that maiden's cheek, where wide
The blushes spread their leaves, to hide
The broken heart which such supplied ;--
    She sought the pair of May-day,
        And to the old one saith,
        " Let thy dart, stedfast Death,
    Cure a forsaken lady ;
        Its point is but for those who'd fly,
        Winged and all soul, into the sky."

## THE RUNAWAY.

Has no one seen my heart of you?
　My heart has run away;
And, if you catch him, ladies, do
　Return him me, I pray.
On earth he is no more, I hear,
　Upon the land or sea;
For the women found the rogue so queer,
　They sent him back to me.
In heaven there is no purchaser
　For such strange ends and odds,
Says a Jew, who goes to Jupiter
　To buy and sell old gods.
So there's but one place more to search,
　That's not genteel to tell,
Where demonesses go to church :—
　So Christians fair, farewell.

## SONG ON THE WATER.

### I.

As mad sexton's bell, tolling
　For earth's loveliest daughter,
Night's dumbness breaks rolling
　　Ghostlily :
　So our boat breaks the water
　　Witchingly.

### II.

As her look the dream troubles
Of her tearful-eyed lover,

So our sails in the bubbles
  Ghostlily
Are mirrored, and hover
  Moonily.


## ALPINE SPIRIT'S SONG.

### I.

O'ER the snow, through the air, to the mountain,
  With the antelope, with the eagle, ho !
  With a bound, with a feathery row,
To the side of the icy fountain,
  Where the gentians blue-belled blow.
Where the storm-sprite, the rain-drops counting,
  Cowers under the bright rainbow,
    Like a burst of midnight fire,
    Singing shoots my fleet desire,
    Winged with the wing of love,
    Earth below and stars above.

### II.

Let me rest on the snow, never pressed
  But by chamois light and by eagle fleet,
  Where the hearts of the antelope beat
'Neath the light of the moony cresset,
  Where the wild cloud rests his feet,
And the scented airs caress it
  From the alpine orchis sweet :
    And about the Sandalp lone
    Voices airy breathe a tone,
    Charming, with the sense of love,
    Earth below and stars above.

### III.

Through the night, like a dragon from Pilate
 Out of murky cave, let us cloudy sail
 Over lake, over bowery vale,
As a chime of bells, at twilight
 In the downy evening gale,
Passes swimming tremulously light;
 Till we reach yon rocky pale
  Of the mountain crowning all,
  Slumber there by waterfall,
  Lonely like a spectre's love,
  Earth beneath, and stars above.


## SONG :

### TRANSLATED FROM THE GERMAN OF WALTHER VON DER VOGELWEIDE.

### I.

UNDER the lime-tree on the daisied ground,
 Two that I know of made their bed ;
There you may see, heaped and scattered round,
 Grass and blossoms, broken and shed,
All in a thicket down in the dale ;
   Tandaradei—
Sweetly sang the nightingale.

### II.

Ere I set foot in the meadow, already
 Someone was waiting for somebody ;
There was a meeting—O gracious Lady !
 There is no pleasure again for me.

Thousands of kisses there he took,—
    Tandaradei—
See my lips, how red they look !

### III.

Leaf and blossom he had pulled and piled
  For a couch, a green one, soft and high ;
·And many a one hath gazed and smiled,
  Passing the bower and pressed grass by ;
And the roses crushed hath seen,—
    Tandaradei—
Where I laid my head between.

### IV.

In this love passage, if any one had been there,
  How sad and shamed should I be !
But what were we a doing alone among the green
    there,
  No soul shall ever know except my love and me,
And the little nightingale.—
    Tandaradei—
She, I think, will tell no tale.

## SONG OF THE STYGIAN NAIADES.

### I.

PROSERPINE may pull her flowers,
  Wet with dew or wet with tears,
  Red with anger, pale with fears,
Is it any fault of ours,
If Pluto be an amorous king,
  And comes home nightly, laden,

Underneath his broad bat-wing,
  With a gentle, mortal maiden?
Is it so, Wind, is it so?
All that you and I do know
Is, that we saw fly and fix
'Mongst the reeds and flowers of Styx,
        Yesterday,
Where the Furies made their hay
For a bed of tiger cubs,
A great fly of Beelzebub's,
The bee of hearts, which mortals name
Cupid, Love, and Fie for shame.

## II.

Proserpine may weep in rage,
  But, ere I and you have done
  Kissing, bathing in the sun,
What I have in yonder cage,
Bird or serpent, wild or tame,
  She shall guess and ask in vain ;
  But, if Pluto does't again,
It shall sing out loud his shame.
  What hast caught then?  What hast caught?
  Nothing but a poet's thought,
  Which so light did fall and fix
  'Mongst the reeds and flowers of Styx,
        Yesterday,
Where the Furies made their hay
For a bed of tiger cubs,—
A great fly of Beelzebub's,
The bee of hearts, which mortals name
Cupid, Love, and Fie for shame.

## THE LILY OF THE VALLEY.

WHERE the hare-bells are ringing
  Their peal of sunny flowers,
And a bird of merry soul
  Sings away the birthday hours
  Of the valley-lily low,
  Opening, dewily and slow,
  Petals, dear to young and fair
  For the prophecy they bear
    Of the coming roses—
The free bold bird of merry soul
Amidst his leaves cannot control
  His triumphant love of spring.

Thou bird of joyous soul,
Why can'st thou not control
  Thy triumphant love of spring?
I know that thou dost rally
  Thy spirit proud to sing,
Because to-day is born
  The lily of the valley.
Oh! rather should'st thou mourn;
  For that flower so meek and low,
    Born with its own death-bell,
    Only cometh to foretell
      Unpitying winter's doom,
  Who in scorn doth lay it low
    In the tomb.

  Vain is all its prayer,
It may flatter, as it will,

The ungentle hours
With its ring of toying flowers;
Unrelenting they must kill
With their scornful breath,
For the very petals fair,
Which the destined flower uncloses
In its innocence,
To plead for its defence,
By the prophecy they bear
Of the coming roses,
Sign the warrant for its death.


## A LAMENT.

In the twilight, silent smiled
All alone the daisy's eyelid,
Fringed with pink-tipped petals piled.
—In the morning 'twas no more;
In its place a gout of gore.
Break of day was break of heart,
Since, dear maiden, dead thou art.


## DIRGE.

Let dew the flowers fill;
No need of fell despair,
Though to the grave you bear
One still of soul—but now too still,
One fair—but now too fair.

For, beneath your feet, the mound,
And the waves, that play around,
Have meaning in their grassy, and their watery,
    smiles ;
And, with a thousand sunny wiles,
    Each says, as he reproves,
    Death's arrow oft is Love's.


## EPITAPH.

THE form's divinity, the heart's best grace,
  Where are they? Have they their immortal
    throne
Upon thy maiden's thought, and peerless face,
  Thou cool-eyed reader? Yet, beneath this stone
Dust lies, weeds grow : and this is the remain
Of one best union of that deathless twain.


## THE TREE OF LIFE.

THERE is a mighty, magic tree,
That holds the round earth and the sea
In its branches like a net :
Its immortal trunk is set
Broader than the tide of night
With its star-tipped billows bright :
Human thought doth on it grow,
Like the barren misletoe
On an old oak's forehead-skin.
Ever while the planets spin

Their blue existence, that great plant
Shall nor bud nor blossom want;
Summer, winter, night and day,
It must still its harvest pay;
Ever while the night grows up
Along the wall of the wide sky,
And the thunder-bee sweeps by,
On its brown, wet wing, to dry
Every day-star's crystal cup
Of its yellow summer:—still
At the foot of heaven's hill,
With fruit and blossom flush and rife,
Stays that tree of Human Life.
Let us mark yon newest bloom
Heaving through the leafy gloom;
Now a pinkish bud it grows
Scentless, bloomless; slow unclose
Its outer pages to the sun,
Opened, but not yet begun.
Its first leaf is infancy,
Pencilled pale and tenderly,
Smooth its cheek and mild its eye:
Now it swells, and curls its head,—
Little infancy is shed.
Broader childhood is the next—

  *   *   *   *

## THE NEW-BORN STAR.

THE world is born to-day!
 What is the world?—Behold the wonder:
 With a mighty thunder,
'Round the sun, it rolls this way;

And its shadow falls afar
  Over many a star,
And the interstellar vale,
Through which some aged, patient globe,
(Whose gaunt sides no summers robe,)
    Like a prisoner through his grate,
    Shivering in despair doth wait
  For sunbeams broken, old, and pale.


  Bounding, like its own fleet deer
  Down a hill, behold a sphere !
  Now a mountain, tall and wide,
  Hanging weighty on its side
  Pulls it down impetuously ;
  Yet the little butterfly,
  Whom the daisy's dew doth glut,
  With his wings' small pages shut,
    Was not stirred.
  Now forests fall, like clouds that gather
  O'er the plain's unruffled weather :
  Burst great rocks, with thunder, out :
  Lakes, their plunged feet about,
  Round, and smooth, and heaving ever,
  An unawakened serpent-river
    Coiled and sleeping.
  Silver changes now are creeping
Down the descending summit of the ball :
  Pastures break, and steadfast land
Sinks, melting :—mighty ocean is at hand.—
Space for eternal waves !  Be strong and wide,
Thou new-born star !  Reflecting all the sky,
And its lone sun, the island-starred tide
    Swells billowing by.

I.                                                    F

At last the dreadful sea is curled
  Behind the nations.    Mark ye now
  The death-intending wrinkles of his brow?
He is the murderous Judas of the world;
     *        *        *        *

  What valley green with stream and tree,
    The fairest, sweetest place,
     *        *        *        *


## THRENODY.

No sunny ray, no silver night,
  Cruelly alight !
Or glare of noon-tide, star of e'en,
  Otherwhere descend !
No violet-eyed green,
  Bare its daisies' yellow end,
The dewy debt receive of any eye !
It is a grave : and *she* doth lie
  'Neath roses' root,
  And the fawn's mossy foot,
Under the sky-lark's floor,
Whose graceful life held every day,—
As lily dew—as dews, the starry ray—
More music, grace, delight than they.
When stars are few let light be here,
  Of the softest, through the boughs
    Berry-laden, sad and few ;
And the wings of one small bird,
His form unseen, his voice unheard—
     *        *        *        *

# LINES

THE hour is starry, and the airs that stray,
Sad wanderers from their golden home of day,
On night's black mountain, melt and fade away
In sorrow that is music.   Some there be
Make them blue pillows on Geneva's sea,
And sleep upon their best-loved planet's shade :
And every herb is sleeping in the glade ;—
They have drunk sunshine and the linnet's song,
Till every leaf's soft sleep is dark and strong.
Or was there ever sound, or can what was
Now be so dead?  Although no flowers or grass
Grow from the corpse of a deceased sound,
Somewhat, methinks, should mark the air around
Its dying place and tomb,
A gentle music, or a pale perfume :
For hath it not a body and a spirit,
A noise and meaning? and, when one doth hear it
Twice born, twice dying, doubly found and lost,
That second self, that echo, is its ghost.
But even the dead are all asleep this time,
And not a grave shakes with the dreams of crime :—
The earth is full of chambers for the dead,
And every soul is quiet in his bed ;
Some who have seen their bodies moulder away,
Antediluvian minds,—most happy they,
Who have no body but the beauteous air,
No body but their minds.   Some wretches are

Now lying with the last and only bone
Of their old selves, and that one worm alone
That ate their heart : some, buried just, behold
Their weary flesh, like an used mansion, sold
Unto a stranger, and see enter it
The earthquake winds and waters of the pit,
Or children's spirits in its holes to play.

*    *    *    *

## STANZAS.

### (FROM THE IVORY GATE.)

THE mighty thoughts of an old world
Fan, like a dragon's wing unfurled,
    The surface of my yearnings deep ;
And solemn shadows then awake,
Like the fish-lizard in the lake,
    Troubling a planet's morning sleep.

My waking is a Titan's dream,
Where a strange sun, long set, doth beam
    Through Montezuma's cypress bough :
Through the fern wilderness forlorn
Glisten the giant harts' great horn,
    And serpents vast with helmed brow.

The measureless from caverns rise
With steps of earthquake, thunderous cries,
    And graze upon the lofty wood ;
The palmy grove, through which doth gleam
Such antediluvian ocean's stream,
    Haunts shadowy my domestic mood.

*    *    *    *

## LINES WRITTEN IN SWITZERLAND.

WHAT silence drear in England's oaky forest,
Erst merry with the redbreast's ballad song
Or rustic roundelay ! No hoof-print on the sward,
Where sometime danced Spenser's equestrian verse
Its mazy measure ! Now by pathless brook
Gazeth alone the broken-hearted stag,
And sees no tear fall in from pitiful eye
Like kindest Shakespeare's. We, who marked
        how fell
Young Adonais, sick of vain endeavour
Larklike to live on high in tower of song ;
And looked still deeper thro' each other's eyes
At every flash of Shelley's dazzling spirit,
Quivering like dagger on the breast of night,—
That seemed some hidden natural light reflected
Upon time's scythe, a moment and away ;
We, who have seen Mount Rydal's snowy head
Bound round with courtly jingles ; list so long
Like old Orion for the break of morn,
Like Homer blind for sound of youthful harp ;
And, if a wandering music swells the gale,
'Tis some poor, solitary heartstring burst.
Well, Britain ; let the fiery Frenchman boast
That at the bidding of the charmer moves
Their nation's heart, as ocean 'neath the moon
Silvered and soothed. Be proud of Manchester,
Pestiferous Liverpool, Ocean-Avernus,
Where bullying blasphemy, like a slimy lie,
Creeps to the highest church's pinnacle,

And glistening infects the light of heaven.
O flattering likeness on a copper coin !
Sit still upon your slave-raised cotton ball,
With upright toasting fork and toothless cat :
The country clown still holds her for a lion.
The voice, the voice ! when the affrighted herds
Dash heedless to the edge of craggy abysses,
And the amazed circle of scared eagles
Spire to the clouds, amid the gletscher clash
When avalanches fall, nation-alarums,—
But clearer, though not loud, a voice is heard
Of proclamation or of warning stern.
    Yet, if I tread out of the Alpine shade,
And once more weave the web of thoughtful verse,
Nay no vainglorious motive break my silence,
Since I have sate unheard so long, in hope
That mightier and better might assay
The potent spell to break, which has fair Truth
Banished so drear a while from mouths of song.
Though genius, bearing out of other worlds
New freights of thought from fresh-discovered
        mines,
Be but reciprocated love of Truth :
Witness kind Shakespeare, our recording angel,
Newton, whose thought rebuilt the universe,
And Galileo, broken-hearted seer,
Who, like a moon attracted naturally,
Kept circling round the central sun of Truth.
Not in the popular playhouse, or full throng
Of opera-gazers longing for deceit ;
Not on the velvet day-bed, novel-strewn,
Or in the interval of pot and pipe ;
Not between sermon and the scandalous paper,

May verse like this ere hope an eye to feed on't.
But if there be, who, having laid the loved
Where they may drop a tear in roses' cups,
With half their hearts inhabit other worlds ;
If there be any—ah ! were there but few—
Who watching the slow lighting up of stars,
Lonely at eve, like seamen sailing near
Some island-city where their dearest dwell,
Cannot but guess in sweet imagining,—
Alas ! too sweet, doubtful, and melancholy,—
Which light is glittering from their loved one's
        home :
Such may perchance, with favourable mind,
Follow my thought along its mountainous path.
    Now then to Caucasus, the cavernous.—

    ＊    ＊    ＊    ＊

## DOOMSDAY.

IF I can raise one ghost, why I will raise
And call up doomsday from behind the east.
Awake then, ghostly doomsday !
Throw up your monuments, ye buried men
That lie in ruined cities of the wastes !
Ye battle fields, and woody mountain sides,
Ye lakes and oceans, and ye lava floods
That have o'erwhelmed great cities, now roll back !
And let the sceptred break their pyramids,
An earthquake of the buried shake the domes
Of arched cathedrals, and o'erturn the forests,
Until the grassy mounds and sculptured floors,
The monumental statues, hollow rocks,
The paved churchyard, and the flowery mead,

And ocean's billowy sarchophagi,
Pass from the bosoms of the rising people
Like clouds !  Enough of stars and suns immortal
Have risen in heaven : to-day, in earth and sea
Riseth mankind.  And first, yawn deep and wide,
Ye marble palace-floors,
And let the uncoffined bones, which ye conceal,
Ascend, and dig their purple murderers up,
Out of their crowned death.   Ye catacombs
Open your gates, and overwhelm the sands
With an eruption of the naked millions,
Out of old centuries !   The buried navies
Shall hear the call, and shoot up from the sea,
Whose wrecks shall knock against the hollow
        mountains,
And wake the swallowed cities in their hearts.
Forgotten armies rattle with their spears
Against the rocky walls of their sepulchres :
An earthquake of the buried shakes the pillars
Of the thick-sown cathedrals ; guilty forests,
Where bloody spades have dug 'mid nightly storms ;
The muddy drowning-places of the babes ;
The pyramids, and bony hiding places,

          *          *          *          *

" Thou rainbow on the tearful lash of doomsday's
        morning star
Rise quick, and let me gaze into that planet deep
        and far,
        As into a loved eye ;
Or I must, like the fiery child of the Vesuvian womb,
Burst with my flickering ghost abroad, before the
        sun of doom
        Rolls up the spectre sky."

A lowly mound, at stormy night, sent up this
      ardent prayer
  Out of a murderer's grave, a traitor's nettly bed,
And the deeds of him, more dread than Cain,
      whose wickedness lay there,
  All mankind hath heard or read.

" Oh doomsday, doomsday come ! thou creative
      morn
Of graves in earth, and under sea, all teeming at
      the horn
      Of angels fair and dread.
As thou the ghosts shalt waken, so I, the ghost,
      wake thee ;
For thy rising sun and I shall rise together from the sea,
      The eldest of the dead."

So crying, oe'r the billowy main, an old ghost strode
      To a churchyard on the shore,
O'er whose ancient corpse the billowy main of ships
      had ebbed and flowed,
      Four thousand years or more.
      *      *      *      *

"World, wilt thou yield thy spirits up, and be
      convulsed and die?
And, as I haunt the billowy main, thy ghost shall
      haunt the sky,
      A pale unheeded star.
Oh doomsday, doomsday, when wilt thou dawn at
      length for me ? "
So having prayed in moonlight waves, beneath the
      shipwrecked sea,
      In spectral caverns far.
      *      *      *      *

## THRENODY.

FAR away,
        As we hear
The song of wild swans winging
        Through the day,
The thought of him, who is no more, comes ringing
        On my ear.

        Gentle fear
        On the breast
Of my memory comes breaking,
        Near and near,
As night winds' murmurous music waking
        Seas at rest.

        As the blest
        Tearful eye
Sees the sun, behind the ocean,
        Red i' th' west,
Grow pale, and in changing hues and fading motion
        Wane and die :

        So do I
        Wake or dream
*          *          *

# POEMS

## HITHERTO UNPUBLISHED

[Now printed for the first time, from the MSS. in the possession of Mr. Robert Barrett Browning. Several of these lyrics appear to have been intended for insertion into " Death's Jest-Book."]

## THE OLD GHOST.

VER the water an old ghost strode
   To a churchyard on the shore,
   And over him the waters had flowed
   A thousand years or more,
And pale and wan and weary
  Looked never a sprite as he ;
For it's lonely and it's dreary
  The ghost of a body to be
  That has mouldered away in the sea.

Over the billows the old ghost stepped,
  And the winds in mockery sung ;
For the bodiless ghost would fain have wept
  Over the maiden that lay so young
'Mong the thistles and toadstools so hoary.
  And he begged of the waves a tear,
But they shook upwards their moonlight glory,
  And the shark looked on with a sneer
  At his yearning desire and agony.

# WRITTEN IN ALBUM AT CLIFTON;
## MARCH, 1828.

LONG have I racked my brains for rhymes to please,
But vainly, for the time doth grow upon me,
And throw the lights and shadows of reality
Thro' my mind's cavern, melting in its glare
The fairy-like inhabitants of twilight
Which I essayed to summon.   Even so
It came to pass, as I have heard it told,
As once a lady's grace and gentleness,
That shed soft beauty over every one
Standing around her,—like to spirits summoned
That must so wait and gaze, but dared not step
Within the circled halo of the charmer,—
Lent to an almost unknown traveller
A book whose leaves are heavy with the music
Of poetry such as she loved to read,
For poetry was her life's element
Which she shook from her, lightly breaking up
The current of men's thought, wherein this world
Was pictured drearily, into fair dimples,
As doth a curled swan silently roving
Thro' the reflection of a haunted palace
Upon a musically enchanted stream.
And on those pages where her eye would dwell
She had permitted the world-wandering stranger
To leave a token of his poor existence:
And now, enclosed in his guest-chamber,
Holding the magic volume which contained
The charms to raise the memory of the gone

Out of the night that had closed over them,
The Traveller, grateful for so sweet a task,
Fain would have spellbound Fiction's fairest shapes,
And sent them captive to pay homage there.
But all in vain : the truth was restless in him,
And shook his visionary fabrics down,
As one who had been buried long ago
And now was called up by a necromancer
To answer dreadful questions.   So compelled,
He left the way of fiction and wrote thus :
" Woe unto him whose fate hath thwarted him,
Whose life has been 'mongst such as were not born,
To cherish in his bosom reverence,
And the calm awe that comforteth the heart
And lulls the yearnings of hope unfulfilled :
Such have I been.   And woe again to him
Who, in too late an hour, presumptuously
O'erhears a wish confessing to his soul,
And must dismiss it to his discontent
With scorn and laughter.   Woe again to me !
For now I hear even such an anxious voice
Crying in my soul's solitude, and bewailing
That I had never in my childhood known
The bud of this manifold beauteousness,
And seen each leaf turn of its tender hinge
Until the last few parted scarce, and held
Deep in their midst a heaven-reflecting gem ;
For then I might—oh vain and flattering wish !—
I might have stood, tho' last, among the friends
Where I am now the last among the strangers,
And not have passed away, as now I must,
Into forgetfulness, into the cold
Of the open, homeless world without a hope,

Unless it be of pardon for these words:
For what is't to the moon that every drop
Of flower-held rain reflects and gazes on her !
Her destiny is in the starry heavens,
Theirs here upon the ground, and she doth set,
Leaving her shadow no more to delight them,
And cometh ne'er again till they are fled.
So is't with me.   Yet to have seen, tho' seldom,
And to have fed me on that beauty's light,
And to have been allowed to trace these thoughts,
Are undeserved favours from my fortune."—

Such was the import of his lines, which many
Would have rejected with a scornful smile,
But if she smiled, smiled pity.   She was gentle;
Read and forgave, and never thought again
On the presumptuous stranger and his lines.
Away !   I should have told a better tale.
Forgive, and shut these pages up for ever.

## SONNET TO ZOË KING.

LEAF after leaf, like a magician's book,
Unfolds the Universe, and needs we now,
  Cousin of mine (while the whole world doth look
Our shoulders over with its rocky brow),
  In turn our living story must transact
Upon the surface of its earthen pages ;
  Whence the still shade of our most needless act
Shall paint itself with iron syllables
  In the arched sight of unawakened ages ;

Therefore 'tis ours, and his who with us dwells
  Beneath the roof of the same starry hour,
Both in his own and in the general mind,
Which is the world, all truth and good to find,
  And finding practise to his end of power.

    *Feb.* 29, 1824.


## FRAGMENT.

FOLLY hath now turned out of door
Mankind and Fate, who were before
  Jove's Harlequin and Clown ;
The World's no stage, no tavern more—
  Its sign the Fool's ta'en down.
    With poppy rain and cypress dew
    Weep all, for all who laughed at you,
    For goose grass is no medicine more,
    But the owl's brown eye's the sky's new blue.
        Heigho ! Foolscap !


## THE FLOWERY ALCHEMIST.

  HIST, oh hist !
My pretty pale young violet,
  Thy moony cheek uncover ;
Lift that hood of fallen sky,
  And my lips once more I'll wet
Against the dew-ball of thine eye.
        Hist, oh hist !

I.                                          G

So a leafy whisper said
Underneath a sweet-briar shade.
  Guess the lady-blossom's lover !
'Twas the flowery Alchymist,
  A stinging, gay, intriguing fellow,
  The wildest bee in black and yellow.

  Hist, oh hist !
My pretty pale young violet !
  Glowworm's lightning blind me
When I leave my bud's embrace,
  When I traitorously forget
Thy cerulean baby's grace.
      Hist, oh hist !

The very next night he told the tale
To a little lily of the vale,
  And the poor young violet died of shame.
Oh ! fie, thou flowery Alchymist,
  Thou stinging, gay, intriguing fellow,
  Thou wildest bee in black and yellow !


## FRAGMENT.

A VEINED petal closes over
    A dewy spark
    Ere Eve is dark,
And starry fireflies flit and hover,
    Dreams of the Rose,
    O'er its repose ;
So bend thy head, and sleep awhile
In the Moon's visionary smile.

# LORD ALCOHOL.

### I.

WHO tames the lion now?
Who smoothes Jove's wrinkles now?
Who is the reckless wight
  That in the horrid middle
Of the deserted night
Doth play upon man's brain,
  As on a wanton fiddle,
The mad and magic strain,
The reeling, tripping sound,
To which the world goes round?
  Sing heigh! ho! diddle!
        And then say—
Love, quotha, Love? nay, nay!
It is a spirit fine
Of ale or ancient wine,
    Lord Alcohol, the drunken fay,
        Lord Alcohol alway!

### II.

Who maketh the pipe-clay man
Think all that nature can?
Who dares the gods to flout,
  Lay fate beneath the table,
And maketh him stammer out
  A thousand monstrous things,
  For history a fable,
  Dish-clouts for kings?

And sends the world along
Singing a ribald song
  Of heigho ! Babel?
      Who, I pray—
Love, quotha, Love? nay, nay !
It is a spirit fine
Of ale or ancient wine,
  Lord Alcohol, the drunken fay,
      Lord Alcohol alway.

## THE OVIPAROUS TAILOR.

  WEE, wee tailor,
  Nobody was paler
  Than wee, wee tailor ;
And nobody was thinner.
Hast thou mutton-chops for dinner,
My small-beer sinner,
  My starveling rat,—but haler,—
  Wee, wee tailor ?

Below his starving garret
Lived an old witch and a parrot,—
  Wee, wee tailor,—
Cross, horrid, and uncivil,
For her grandsire was the Devil,
Or a chimney-sweeper evil ;
She was sooty, too, but paler,—
  Wee, wee tailor.

Her sooty hen laid stale eggs,
And then came with his splay legs,—
  Wee, wee tailor, -

And stole those eggs for dinner ;
Then would old witch begin her
Damnations on the sinner,—
  " May the thief lay eggs,—but staler ; "
    Wee, wee tailor.

Wee, wee tailor,
Witch watched him like a jailor.
  Wee, wee tailor
Did all his little luck spill.
Tho' he swallowed many a muck's pill,
Yet his mouth grew like a duck's bill,
  Crowed like a hen,—but maler,—
    Wee, wee tailor.

Near him did cursèd doom stick,
As he perched upon a broomstick, —
  Wee, wee tailor.
It lightened, rained, and thundered,
And all the doctors wondered
When he layed about a hundred
  Gallinaceous eggs,—but staler,—
    Wee, wee tailor.
A hundred eggs laid daily ;
No marvel he looked palely,—
  Wee, wee tailor.

Witch let folks in to see some
Poach'd tailor's eggs ; to please 'em
He must cackle on his besom,
  Till Fowl-death did prevail o'er
    Wee, wee tailor.

## SILENUS IN PROTEUS.

OH those were happy days, heaped up with wine-
    skins,
And ivy-wreathed and thyrsus-swinging days,
Swimming like streamy-tressed wanton Bacchantes,
When I was with thee, and sat kingly on thee,
My ass of asses.   Then quite full of wine—
Morning, eve—and leaning on a fawn,
Still pretty steady, and on t'other side
Some vinous-lipped nymph of Ariadne,
Her bosom a soft cushion for my right :
Half dreaming and half waking, both in bliss,
I sat upon my ass and laughed at Jove.
But thou art dead, my dapple, and I too
Shall ride thee soon about the Elysian meadow,
Almost a skeleton as well as thou.
And why, oh dearest, couldst not keep thy legs
That sacred hair, sacred to sacred me ?
Was this thy gratitude for pats and fondlings,
To die like any other mortal ass ?
Was it for this, oh son of Semele,
I taught thee then, a little tumbling one,
To suck the goatskin oftener than the goat ?


## SONG.

THE Snake is come out,
    And the bee is about,
In the sunny delight of Hymettus ;

O would I were he,
The gay dappled bee,
For then the Narcissus would let us
Drink out of her bosom,
Ambrosian blossom,
To the health of her neighbour, the Olive,
The first drop of spring ;
Oh ! happy the thing
That in Greece the mellifluous can so live.

The green frog of the ditch
Pours his love loud and rich,
Coaxing the water-maid's shoulder,
And from round golden eyes
Darts in amorous wise
A sheaf of love's bee-stings like arrows ;
And Love's in the wood,
In a goat-footed mood,
Dancing with Pan and his fellows ;
So my nymphs may beware
Of their treasury rare
Of bosoms and cheeks the sun mellows.

But here O ! ho ! cold,
Snowy, mountainous, old,
Is the earth of the barbarous island.
    *     *     *     *     *

# THE BRIDES' TRAGEDY.

["The Brides' Tragedy. By Thomas Lovell Beddoes, of Pembroke College, Oxford. London: printed for F. C. and J. Rivington, St. Paul's Churchyard, and Waterloo-Place, Pall-Mall. 1822." This play was reprinted in 1851, and now appears for the third time.]

TO

# THE REV. H. CARD, M.A., F.R.S. F.A.S.,

## ETC. ETC. ETC.

MY DEAR SIR,

As you have, in a late publication,[1] which dis-
plays your usual learning and judgment, mentioned
this performance in terms, perhaps dictated by
friendship rather than critical impartiality, I must
beg to inscribe it to your name.

There are many prejudices with which a playwright has to contend, on his first appearance,
more especially if he court the reader in lieu of the
spectator; and it is so great an effort to give up
any established topic of condolement, that we can
hardly yet expect those, who call themselves " the
critics," to abandon their favourite complaint of
the degeneracy which characterizes the efforts of
contemporary tragic writers. But let any unpre-
judiced person turn to the productions even of the
present year; let him candidly examine the anonymous play, " The Court of Tuscany," and compare
its best scenes with the master-pieces of Rowe or
Otway; let him peruse Allan Cunningham's poetical drama, which has won the applause of the
highest literary authority of the day; let him dwell

[1] See Dissertation on the Herefordshire Beacon, Note.

upon the energetic grandeur and warlike animation
which Croly has so successfully displayed in pour-
traying the restless spirit of Catiline ; and I think
his verdict will place this age not the last among
those which have done honour to the British stage.

These instances are sufficient to attest the
flourishing condition of dramatic literature, but;
alas ! we must seek them in the closet, not in their
proper home, the populous theatre, for there we
shall meet with a sight, sufficient to deter the
boldest adventurer from hazarding the representa-
tion of his best and most vaunted piece, our
countrymen barely enduring the poetry of Shakespeare as the vehicle of a fashionable song or a
gaudy pageant.   Even the theatre itself however
may appear "not yet enslaved, not wholly vile,"
as long as the classic taste of Milman, the plaintive
sweetness of Barry Cornwall, and the frank nature
of Knowles, linger, like flowers upon the Muse's
grave.   But they have almost deserted the public
haunt, and England can hardly boast anything
that deserves to be called a national stage.

The following scenes were written, as you well
know, exclusively for the closet, founded upon facts,
which occurred at Oxford, and are well detailed and
illustrated by an interesting ballad in a little volume
of Poems, lately published at Oxford, entitled the
Midland Minstrel, by Mr. Gillet : and may thus
be succinctly narrated.

The Manciple of one of the Colleges early in
the last century had a very beautiful daughter,
who was privately married to a student without
the knowledge of the parents on either side.

During the long vacation subsequent to this union the husband was introduced to a young lady, who was at the same time proposed as his bride : absence, the fear of his father's displeasure, the presence of a lovely object, and, most likely, a natural fickleness of disposition overcame any regard he might have cherished for his ill-fated wife, and finally he became deeply enamoured of her unconscious rival. In the contest of duties and desires, which was the consequence of this passion, the worse part of man prevailed, and he formed and executed a design almost unparalleled in the annals of crime.

His second nuptials were at hand when he returned to Oxford, and to her who was now an obstacle to his happiness. Late at night he prevailed upon his victim to accompany him to a lone spot in the *Divinity Walk*, and there murdered and buried her. The wretch escaped detection, and the horrid deed remained unknown till he confessed it on his death-bed. The remains of the unfortunate girl were dug up in the place described, and the Divinity Walk was deserted and demolished as haunted ground. Such are the outlines of a *Minor's Tragedy*.

My age, it will be said, is a bad excuse for the publication of a faulty poem; be it so: secure of your approbation, I can meet with a careless smile the frown of him who reads only to condemn.

I am, my dear Sir,

Your's most sincerely,

Thomas Lovell Beddoes.

## DRAMATIS PERSONÆ.

The DUKE.
LORD ERNEST.
HESPERUS, his Son.
ORLANDO.
CLAUDIO.
MORDRED.
HUBERT.
A HUNTSMAN.
BOY, Page to Orlando.
JAILOR.

OLIVIA, Sister to Orlando.
VIOLETTA, her Companion.
LENORA, Wife of Mordred.
FLORIBEL, her Daughter.

*Lords, Citizens, Attendants, Guards, &c.*

# THE BRIDES' TRAGEDY.

## ACT I.

### SCENE I. *A garden.*

#### HESPERUS *alone.*

NOW Eve has strewn the sun's wide bil-
    lowy couch
    With rose-red feathers moulted from
    her wing,
Still scanty-sprinkled clouds, like lagging sheep,
Some golden-fleeced, some streaked with delicate
    pink,
Are creeping up the welkin, and behind
The wind, their boisterous shepherd, whistling
    drives them,
From the drear wilderness of night to drink
Antipodean noon. At such a time,
While to wild melody fantastic dreams
Dance their gay morrice in the midmost air,
And sleepers' truant fancies fly to join them ;
While that winged song, the restless nightingale
Turns her sad heart to music, sweet it is
Unseen on the moss-cushioned sward to lean,
And into some coy ear pour out the soul
In sighs and whispers.

*Enter* FLORIBEL.

So late, Floribel?
Nay, since I see that arch smile on thy cheek
Rippling so prettily, I will not chide,
Although the breeze and I have sighed for you
A dreary while, and the veiled Moon's mild eye
Has long been seeking for her loveliest nymph.
Come, come, my love, or shall I call you bride?

   *Flor.* E'en what you will, so that you hold me
     dear.

   *Hesp.* Well, both my love and bride; see, here's
     a bower
Of eglantine with honeysuckles woven,
Where not a spark of prying light creeps in,
So closely do the sweets enfold each other.
'Tis Twilight's home; come in, my gentle love,
And talk to me.   So! I've a rival here;
What's this that sleeps so sweetly on your neck?

   *Flor.* Jealous so soon, my Hesperus? Look
     then,
It is a bunch of flowers I pulled for you:
Here's the blue violet, like Pandora's eye,
When first it darkened with immortal life.

   *Hesp.* Sweet as thy lips. Fie on those taper
     fingers,
Have they been brushing the long grass aside
To drag the daisy from it's hiding-place,
Where it shuns light, the Danäe of flowers,
With gold up-hoarded on its virgin lap?

   *Flor.* And here's a treasure that I found by
     chance,
A lily of the valley; low it lay

Over a mossy mound, withered and weeping
As on a fairy's grave.

  *Hesp.*      Of all the posy
Give me the rose, though there's a tale of blood
Soiling its name. In elfin annals old
'Tis writ, how Zephyr, envious of his love,
(The love he bare to Summer, who since then
Has weeping visited the world;) once found
The baby Perfume cradled in a violet;
('Twas said the beauteous bantling was the child
Of a gay bee, that in his wantonness
Toyed with a pea-bud in a lady's garland;)
The felon winds, confederate with him,
Bound the sweet slumberer with golden chains,
Pulled from the wreathed laburnum, and together
Deep cast him in the bosom of a rose,
And fed the fettered wretch with dew and air.
At length his soul, that was a lover's sigh,
Waned from his body, and the guilty blossom
His heart's blood stained. The twilight-haunting
   gnat
His requiem whined, and harebells tolled his knell;
And still the bee, in pied velvet dight,
With melancholy song, from flower to flower,
Goes seeking his lost offspring.

  *Flor.*      Take it then,
In its green sheath. What guess you, Hesperus,
I dreamed last night? Indeed it makes me sad,
And yet I think you love me.

  *Hesp.*     By the planet
That sheds its tender blue on lovers' sleeps,
Thou art my sweetest, nay, mine only thought:
And when my heart forgets thee, may yon heaven

 I.                  H

Forget to guard me.

*Flor.*                    Aye, I knew thou didst;
Yet surely mine's a sad and lonely fate
Thus to be wed to secresy; I doubt,
E'en while I know my doubts are causeless tor-
          ments.
Yet I conjure thee, if indeed I hold
Some share in thy affections, cast away
The blank and ugly vizor of concealment,
And, if mine homely breeding do not shame thee,
Let thy bride share her noble father's blessing.

*Hesp.* In truth I will; nay, prithee let me kiss
That naughty tear away; I will, by heaven;
For, though austere and old, my sire must gaze
On thy fair innocence with glad forgiveness.
Look up, my love,
See how yon orb, dressed out in all her beams,
Puts out the common stars, and sails along
The stately Queen of heaven; so shall thy beauties,
But the rich casket of a noble soul,
Shine on the world and bless it.   Tell me now
This frightful vision.

*Flor.*                   You will banter me;
But I'm a simple girl, and oftentimes
In solitude am very, very mournful:
And now I think how silly 'twas to weep
At such an harmless thing: well, you shall hear.
'Twas on a fragrant bank I laid me down,
Laced o'er and o'er with verdant tendrils, full
Of dark-red strawberries.   Anon there came
On the wind's breast a thousand tiny noises,
Like flowers' voices, if they could but speak;
Then slowly did they blend in one sweet strain,

Melodiously divine; and buoyed the soul
Upon their undulations.   Suddenly,
Methought, a cloud swam swanlike o'er the sky,
And gently kissed the earth, a fleecy nest,
With roses, rifled from the cheek of Morn,
Sportively strewn; upon the ethereal couch,
Her fair limbs blending with the enamoured mist,
Lovely above the portraiture of words,
In beauteous languor lay the Queen of Smiles:
In tangled garlands, like a golden haze,
Or fay-spun threads of light, her locks were floating,
And in their airy folds slumbered her eyes,
Dark as the nectar-grape that gems the vines
In the bright orchard of the Hesperides.
Within the ivory cradle of her breast
Gambolled the urchin god, with saucy hand
Dimpling her cheeks, or sipping eagerly
The rich ambrosia of her melting lips:
Beneath them swarmed a bustling mob of Loves,
Tending the sparrow stud, or with bees' wings
Imping their arrows.   Here stood one alone,
Blowing a pyre of blazing lovers' hearts
With bellows full of absence-caused sighs:
Near him his work-mate mended broken vows
With dangerous gold, or strung soft rhymes together
Upon a lady's tress.   Some swelled their cheeks,
Like curling rose-leaves, or the red wine's bubbles,
In petulant debate, gallantly tilting
Astride their darts.   And one there was alone,
Who with wet downcast eyelids threw aside
The remnants of a broken heart, and looked
Into my face and bid me 'ware of love,
Of fickleness, and woe, and mad despair.

*Hesp.* Aye, so he said; and did my own dear
    girl
Deem me a false one for this foolish dream?
I wish I could be angry: hide, distrustful,
Those penitent blushes in my breast, while I
Sing you a silly song old nurses use
To hush their crying babes with.    Tenderly
'Twill chide you.

### *Song.*

    Poor old pilgrim Misery,
      Beneath the silent moon he sate,
    A-listening to the screech owl's cry,
      And the cold wind's goblin prate;
    Beside him lay his staff of yew
      With withered willow twined,
    His scant grey hair all wet with dew,
      His cheeks with grief ybrined;
        And his cry it was ever, alack!
        Alack, and woe is me!

    Anon a wanton imp astray
      His piteous moaning hears,
    And from his bosom steals away
      His rosary of tears:
    With his plunder fled that urchin elf,
      And hid it in your eyes,
    Then tell me back the stolen pelf,
      Give up the lawless prize;
        Or your cry shall be ever, alack!
        Alack, and woe is me!

*Hesp.* Not yet asleep?

*Flor.*      Asleep ! No, I could ever,
Heedless of times and seasons, list to thee.
But now the chilly breeze is sallying out
Of dismal clouds ; and silent midnight walks
Wrapt in her mourning robe. I fear it's time
To separate.

 *Hesp.* So quickly late ! oh cruel, spiteful hours,
Why will ye wing your steeds from happiness,
And put a leaden drag upon your wheels
When grief hangs round our hearts. Soon will we
  meet,
And to part never more.

 *Flor.*      Oh ! that dear never,
It will pay all. Good night, and think of me.

 *Hesp.* Good night, my love ; may music-winged
  sleep
Bind round thy temples with her poppy wreath ;
Soft slumbers to thee.     [*Exeunt.*


## SCENE II.

*A room in Orlando's palace.*

CLAUDIO *and* ORLANDO *meeting.*

 *Orl.* Thanks for thy speed, good Claudio ; is all
  done
As I have ordered ?

 *Clau.*     Could I be unwilling
In the performance of what you command,
I'd say with what regret I led Lord Ernest
Into the prison. My dear lord,
He was your father's friend—

*Orl.*                                    And he is mine.
You must not think Orlando so forgetful
As to abuse the reverence of age,
An age, like his, of piety and virtue;
'Tis but a fraud of kindness, sportive force.

    *Clau.* You joy me much, for now I dare to own
I almost thought it was a cruel deed.

    *Orl.* Nay, you shall hear.   The sums he owed
        my father,
Of which his whole estate is scarce a fourth,
Are never to be claimed, if Hesperus,
His son, be wedded to Olivia.   Now
This Hesperus, you tell me, is a votary,
A too much favoured votary of my goddess,
The Dian of our forests, Floribel;
Therefore I use this show of cruelty,
To scare a rival and to gain a brother.

    *Clau.* Now by the patches on the cheek of the
        moon,
(Is't not a pretty oath?) a good romance;
We'll have't in ballad metre, with a burthen
Of sighs, how one bright glance of a brown damsel
Lit up the tinder of Orlando's heart
In a hot blaze.

    *Orl.*               Enough to kindle up
An altar in my breast!  'Twas but a moment,
And yet I would not sell that grain of time
For thy eternity of heartlessness.

    *Clau.* Well, well.   I can bear nonsense from a
        lover;
Oh, I've been mad threescore and eighteen times
And three quarters; written twenty yards, two
        nails,

An inch and a quarter, cloth measure, of sonnets ;
Wasted as much salt water as would pickle
Leviathan, and sighed enough to set up
Another wind ;——

    *Orl.*          Claudio, I pray thee, leave me ;
I relish not this mockery.

    *Clau.*          Good sir, attend
To my experience.   You've no stock as yet
To set up lover : get yourself a pistol
Without a touch-hole, or at least remember,
If it be whole, to load it with wet powder ;
I've known a popgun, well applied, or even
The flying of a cork, give reputation
To courage and despair.   A gross of garters,
Warranted rotten, will be found convenient

    *Orl.* Now you are troublesome.

    *Clau.*          One precept more ;
Purge and drink watergruel, lanthorn jaws
Are interesting ; fat men can't write sonnets,
And indigestion turns true love to bile.

    *Orl.* 'Tis best to part.   If you desire to serve
      me,
Persuade the boy to sacrifice his passion ;
I'll lead him to Olivia, they were wont
In childhood to be playmates, and some love
May lie beneath the ashes of that friendship,
That needs her breath alone to burst and blaze.

                    [*Exeunt.*

## SCENE III.

*A prison.*

*Enter* Guards *leading* LORD ERNEST *in chains.*

*L. Ern.* I pray you do not pity me.    I feel
A kind of joy to meet Calamity,
My old, old friend again.    Go, tell your lord,
I give him thanks for these his iron bounties.
How now?  I thought you led me to a prison,
A dismal antichamber of the tomb,
Where creatures dwell, whose ghosts but half in-
    habit
Their ruinous flesh-houses ; here is air
As fresh as that the bird of morning sings in,
And shade that scarce is dusk, but just enough
To please the meek and twilight-loving eye
Of lone Religion.    'Tis an hermitage
Where I may sit and and tell my o'erpassed years,
And fit myself for dying.    My old heart
Holds not enough of gratitude to pay
This noble kindness, that in guise of cruelty
Compels me to my good.
    *Guard.*                     I am most glad
That you endure thus cheerfully ; remember
Your son's one word will give you liberty.
    *L. Ern.* I know he would not do me so much
        wrong.
You think, because I'm white with age, I mourn
Such hardships.  See, my hand's as firm and steady
As when I broke my first spear in the wars ;

Alas ! I am so glad, I cannot smile.

   *Guard.* We sorrow thus to leave thee.

   *L. Ern.*                        Sorrow ! man,

It is a woman's game : I cannot play it.

Away ; your whining but provokes my spleen.

   [*As the* Guards *are retiring he bursts into a*
       *harsh laugh: when they have left the stage*
       *he stops short.*]

They're gone and cannot hear me. Now, then,
   now,

Eyes weep away' my life, heart, if thou hast

A pulse to strain, break, break, oh break !

           *Enter* HESPERUS.

                           My son

Come here, I'll tell thee all they've done to me,

How they have scoffed and spurned me, thrown
      me here

In wretched loneliness.

   *Hesp.*               Alas ! my father.

   *L Ern.* Oh set me free, I cannot bear this air.

If thou dost recollect those fearful hours,

When I kept watch beside my precious boy,

And saw the day but on his pale, dear face ;

If thou didst think me, in my gentlest moods,

Patient and mild, and even somewhat kind ;

Oh give me back the pity that I lent,

Pretend at least to love and comfort me.

   *Hesp.* Speak not so harshly ; I'm not rich enough

To pay one quarter of the dues of love,

Yet something I would do. Show me the way,

I will revenge thee well.

   *L. Ern.*            But, whilst thou'rt gone

The dread diseases of the place will come
And kill me wretchedly.   No, I'll be free.
 *Hesp.* Aye, that thou shalt.   I'll do; what will
   I not?
I'll get together all the world's true hearts,
And if they're few, there's spirit in my breast
Enough to animate a thousand dead.
 *L. Ern.*          My son
We need not this; a word of thine will serve.
 *Hesp.* Were it my soul's last sigh I'd give it thee.
 *L. Ern.* Marry.
 *Hesp.*      I—cannot.
 *L. Ern.*        But thou dost not know
Thy best-loved woos thee.   Oft I've stood unseen,
In some of those sweet evenings you remember,
Watching your innocent and beauteous play,
(More innocent because you thought it secret,
More beautiful because so innocent;)
Oh! then I knew how blessed a thing I was
To have a son so worthy of Olivia.
 *Hesp.*          Olivia!
 *L. Ern.* Blush not, though I name your mistress;
You soon shall wed her.     I will wed the plague.
 *Hesp.*
I would not grudge my life, for that's a thing,
A misery, thou gavest me: but to wed
Olivia; there's damnation in the thought.
 *L. Ern.* Come, speak to him, my chains, for
   ye've a voice
To conquer every heart that's not your kin?
Oh! that ye were my son, for then at least
He would be with me.   How I loved him once!
Aye, when I thought him good; but now—Nay, still

He must be good, and I, I have been harsh,
I feel, I have not prized him at his worth :
And yet I think, if Hesperus had erred,
I could have pardoned him, indeed I could.
   *Hesp.* We'll live together.
   *L. Ern.*            No, for I shall die ;
But that's no matter.
   *Hesp.*          Bring the priest, the bride.
Quick, quick. These fetters have infected him
With slavery's sickness. Yet there is a secret,
'Twixt heaven and me, forbids it. Tell me,
     father ;
Were it not best for both to die at once ?
   *L. Ern.* Die ! thou hast spoke a word, that
     makes my heart
Grow sick and wither ; thou hast palsied me
To death. Live thou to wed some worthier maid ;
Know that thy father chose this sad seclusion ;
(Ye rebel lips, why do you call it sad ?)
Should I die soon, think not that sorrow caused it,
But, if you recollect my name, bestow it
Upon your best-loved child, and when you give him
His Grandsire's blessing, add not that he perished
A wretched prisoner.
   *Hesp.*         Stop, or I am made
I know not what,—perhaps a villain. Curse me,
Oh if you love me, curse.
   *L. Ern.*         Aye, thou shalt hear
A father's curse ; if fate hath put a moment
Of pain into thy life ; a sigh, a word,
A dream of woe ; be it transferred to mine ;
And for thy days ; oh ! never may a thought
Of others' sorrow, even of old Ernest's,

Darken their calm, uninterrupted bliss ;
And be thy end—oh ! any thing but mine.

   *Hesp.* Guilt, thou art sanctified in such a cause ;
Guards ; (*they enter*) I am ready.    Let me say't so
     low,
So quickly that it may escape the ear
Of watchful angels ; I will do it all.

   *L. Ern.* There's nought to do ; I've learned to
     love this solitude.
Farewell, my son.    Nay, never heed the fetters ;
We can make shift to embrace.

   *Hesp.*              Lead him to freedom,
And tell your lord I will not,—that's I will.

            [*Exeunt* LORD ERNEST *and* Guards.
Here, fellow ; put your hand upon my mouth
Till they are out of hearing.    Leave me now.
No, stay ; come near me, nearer yet.    Now fix
The close attention of your eyes on mine.

   *Guard.*                  My lord !

   *Hesp.* See'st thou not death in them ?

   *Guard.*               Forbid it, fate.

   *Hesp.* Away ! ill-omened hound ;
I'll be a ghost and play about the graves,
For ghosts can never wed.      [*Exit* Guard.
There, there they go ; my hopes, my youthful
     hopes,
Like ingrate flatterers.    What have I to do
With life ? Ye sickly stars, that look with pity
On this cursed head, be kind and tell the lightning
To scathe me to a cinder ; or if that
Be too much blessing for a child of sin,
But strike me mad, I do not ask for more.
Come from your icy caves, ye howling winds,

Clad in your gloomy panoply of clouds,
And call into your cars, as ye pass o'er
The distant quarters of this tortured world,
Every disease of every clime,
Here shall they banquet on a willing victim ;
Or with one general ague shake the earth,
The pillars of the sky dissolve and burst,
And let the ebon-tiled roof of night
Come tumbling in upon the doomed world :—
Deaf are they still? then death is all a fable,
A pious lie to make man lick his chains
And look for freedom's dawning through his grate.
Why are we tied unto this wheeling globe,
Still to be racked while traitorous Hope stands by,
And heals the wounds that they may gape again ?
Aye to this end the earth is made a ball,
Else crawling to the brink despair would plunge
Into the infinite eternal air,
And leave its sorrows and its sins behind.
Since death will not, come sleep, thou kindred
        power,
Lock up my senses with thy leaden key,
And darken every crevice that admits
Light, life, and misery, if thou canst, for ever. [*Exit.*

## ACT II.

### Scene I.

*A chamber in Orlando's palace.*

*Enter* ORLANDO *to his* Boy *asleep.*

*Orl.* Boy ! he is asleep ;
Oh innocence, how fairly dost thou head
This pure, first page of man.   Peace to thy
    slumbers ;
Sleep, for thy dreams are 'midst the seraphs' harps,
Thy thoughts beneath the wings of holiness,
Thine eyes in paradise.
The day may come, (if haply gentle death
Say not amen to thy short prayer of being,
And lap thee in the bosom of the blest ;)
I weep to think on, when the guilty world
Shall, like a friend, be waiting at thy couch,
And call thee up on ev'ry dawn of crime.
    *Boy (awaking).* Dear master, didst thou call ? I
        will not be
A second time so slothful.
    *Orl.*               Sleep, my boy,
Thy task is light and joyous, to be good.
    *Boy.* Oh !  if I must be good, then give me
        money,
I pray thee, give me some, and you shall find

I'll buy up every tear, and make them scarcer
Than diamonds.

    *Orl.* Beautiful pity, thou shalt have enough ;
But you must give me your last song.

    *Boy.*                    Nay, sir ;
You're wont to say my rhymes are fit for girls,
And lovesick idiots ; I have none you praise
Full of the heat of battle and the chase.

    *Orl.* Sing what you will, I'll like it.


### Song.

A ho !  A ho !
  Love's horn doth blow,
    And he will out a-hawking go.
His shafts are light as beauty's sighs,
And bright as midnight's brightest eyes,
    And round his starry way
The swan-winged horses of the skies,
With summer's music in their manes,
Curve their fair necks to zephyr's reins,
    And urge their graceful play.


A ho !  A ho !
  Love's horn doth blow,
    And he will out a-hawking go.
The sparrows flutter round his wrist,
The feathery thieves that Venus kissed
    And taught their morning song,
The linnets seek the airy list,
And swallows too, small pets of Spring,
Beat back the gale with swifter wing,
    And dart and wheel along.

A ho ! A ho !
  Love's horn doth blow,
    And he will out a-hawking go.
Now woe to every gnat that skips
To filch the fruit of ladies' lips,
        His felon blood is shed ;
And woe to flies, whose airy ships
On beauty cast their anchoring bite,
And bandit wasp, that naughty wight,
        Whose sting is slaughter-red.


*Orl.* Who is thy poet, boy ?
*Boy.*                              I must not tell.
*Orl.* Then I will chide thee for him.   Who first
    drew
Love as a blindfold imp, an earthern dwarf,
And armed him with blunt darts?  His soul was
    kin
To the rough wind that dwells in the icy north,
The dead, cold pedant, who thus dared confine
The universe's soul, for that is Love.
'Tis he that acts the nightingale, the thrush,
And all the living musics, he it is
That gives the lute, the harp, and tabor speech,
That flutters on melodious wings and strikes
The mute and viewless lyres of sunny strings
Borne by the minstrel gales, mimicking vainly
The timid voice, that sent him to my breast,
That voice the wind hath treasured and doth use
When he bids roses open and be sweet.
  *Boy.* Now I could guess.
  *Orl.*                         What, little curious one ?
  *Boy.* The riddle of Orlando's feelings.   Come,

You must not frown.    I know the lawn, the cot,
Aye, and the leaf-veiled lattice.
 *Orl.*      I shall task
Your busy watchfulness.    Bear you this paper,
I would not trust it to a doubtful hand.
  *Boy.* Unto the wood-nymph?    You may think
    the road
Already footed.
 *Orl.*    Go, and prosper then.    [*Exeunt.*


## SCENE II.

*The interior of Mordred's cottage.*

LENORA *and* FLORIBEL.

 *Flor.* My mother, you're too kind, you ought to
    check
These wayward humours.    Oh, I know too well
I'm a poor, foolish, discontented child ;
My heart doth sink when Hesperus is gone,
And leaves me nought but fears.    Forgive me then,
If I have vexed you.
 *Len.*    Dear and gentle soul,
You ne'er offended me, but when you said
You had offended.    When I look on thee,
If there's a thought that moistens in my eye,
Fear, that thy husband cannot match such goodness,
Is looking out there.
 *Flor.*    Fears of Hesperus !
That's not my mother's thought, cast it away :
He is the glass of all good qualities,

 I.             I

And what's a little virtue in all others
Looks into him and sees itself a giant ;
He is a nosegay of the sweets of man,
A dictionary of superlatives ;
He walks about, a music among discords,
A star in night, a prayer 'midst madmen's curses ;
And if mankind, as I do think, were made
To bear the fruit of him, and him alone,
It was a glorious destiny.

*Len.* He is a goodly man, and yet they say
Strange passions sleep within him. There's Orlando,
A gentle suitor ; Floribel, he loved you,
He had no father, I have often wished
What it's too late to tell you.

*Flor.*                              Mother, your Orlando
Is a good gentleman, I wish him well,
But to my husband—We'll not talk of him.
Yet you shall see I can be cool sometimes,
When Hesperus deserves it, as he does
Even now for his delay.

*Len.*                              He's here : I'll leave you,
You shall not quarrel with him for my pleasure.
                                        [*Exit.*


*Enter* HESPERUS.

*Hesp.* Good morrow, Floribel.
*Flor.*   Fair noon to Hesperus ; I knew a youth,
In days of yore, would quarrel with a lark,
If with its joyous matins it foreran
His early pipe beneath his mistress' window ;
Those days are passed ; alas ! for gallantry.
*Hesp.*                              Floribel !
*Flor.* Sir, d'ye know the gentleman ?

Give him my benison and bid him sleep
Another hour, there's one that does not miss him.

*Hesp.* Lady, I came to talk of other things,
To tell you all my secrets : must I wait
Until it fits your humour ?

*Flor.*                    As you please :
(The worst of three bad suitors, and his name
Began with an H.)

*Hesp.* Good morrow then, again.

*Flor.*                    Heaven help you, sir,
And so adieu.

*Hesp.* Madam, you spoke ; you said it, Floribel :
I never thought mine ears a curse before.
Did I not love thee ?   Say, have I not been
The kindest ?

*Flor.*          Yes indeed thou *hast* been.   Now
A month is over.   What would I not give
For those four sevens of days?   But I have lived
      them,
And that's a bliss.   You speak as if I'd lost
The little love you gave your poor one then.

*Hesp.* And you as if you cared not for the loss
Oh Floribel, you'll make me curse the chance
That fashioned this sad clay and made it man ;
It had been happier as the senseless tree
That canopies your sleep.   But Hesperus,
He's but the burthen of a scornful song
Of coquetry ; beware, that song may end
In a death-groan.

  *Flor.* (*sings*).
        The knight he left the maid,
          That knight of fickleness,

> Her's was the blame he said,
> And his the deep distress.

If you are weary of poor Floribel,
Pray be not troubled ; she can do without thee.
Oh Hesperus, come hither, I must weep ;
Say you will love me still, and I'll believe it,
When I forget my folly.
    *Hesp.*          Dear, I do ;
By the bright fountains of those tears I do.
    *Flor.* You don't despise me much? May I look up
And meet no frown ?
    *Hesp.*        Try to look through my breast,
And see my truth.   But, oh ! my Floribel,
Take heed how thou dost look unkindly on me ;
For grey-beards have been kneeling, and with
        prayers
Trying to pluck thee from my bosom ; fairness,
And innocence, and duty league against thee.
Then do't not, sweet, again ; for sometimes strange
And horrid thoughts bring whispers to my soul :
They shall not harm thee, girl.   I meant indeed,
Hard hearted as I was, to have disclosed
A tale of terror ; but I'll back again :
Why, let the old man die.
    *Flor.*         Oh no, no, no ;
We will let no one die, but cherish them
With love like ours, and they will soon be well :
Stay and I'll tell you how to save him.
    *Hesp.*         Thou !
Excellent loveliness
Thou save him !   But I must be gone, or else
Those looks will lure a secret from my breast,

That threatens both.  I'll home and think of some-
    thing.
Meet me to-morrow in the sweet-briar thicket,
When twilight fades to evening.   I'm in haste.
[*Exit.*

  *Flor.*  My better thoughts go with thee.  It is true
He hath too much of human passion in him,
But I will hold him dear, and, if again
My wicked senses grow so cruel quick
As to suspect his kindness, I'll be sure
My eyes have got false sight, my ears false hearing,
And my whole mind's become a rebel traitress.

*Enter* ORLANDO'S Boy.

  *Boy.*  These for fair Floribel ; you are the one
I hear my master talk of, surely, lady ;
And yet his words are feeble shadowers
Of such pure beauty.   Please you read his thoughts.
  *Flor.*  You hold a courtly language for such years ;
But be you 'ware of compliment akin
To falsehood.

    (*Reads.*) *From the sad-souled Orlando.*
Fie sir ; your gifts are dangerous.   Look you here,
As I disperse the wicked syllables
Met in this little parliament of words,
And give them to the light and careless winds,
So do I bid him tear the thoughts of me
Out of his breast, and hold me as a thing
Further from him than misery.
  *Boy.*  It is ungently done,—nay, I must say so,—
To hurt the generous blossoms of his love ;
I am sorry that a hand so beautiful
Can be so fell.

*Flor.*                Boy, thou dost not know
The fears that urge me.   Had my Hesperus
Seen these or thee, I know not what of ill
Must have befallen us.
　*Boy.*                 Lady, you must not weep;
I have a ballad which my master hears
In his sad moods; it has the art to raise
A dimple on the cheek of moody care.
I'll sing it you.
　*Flor.*            Young one, I almost love thee.

*[Kisses him.*


*Enter* HESPERUS.

*Hesp.* Why Floribel,—Girl! Painted fickleness!
Madam, I'm rude; but Hesperus did not think
He could intrude on—what was Floribel.
　*Flor.*               . Nor doth he ever.
　*Hesp.* If he does not now,
Be sure he won't again.   Oh girl, girl, girl,
Thou'st killed my heart: I thought thee once, good
　　fool,
I will not tell thee what, thou'lt laugh at me.
　*Flor.*                      By heaven!
　*Hesp.* Don't name it: do not be forsworn.
But why should I regard thy words or oaths?
　*Flor.* Hesperus, Hesperus!
　*Hesp.*               Nay, I should be sorry
To cheat the longing boy; he fills thine arms
Excellent well, believe it.   Urchin, seek me
When that mis-featured butter-print of thine
Is bearded; I will trim thee with a sword.
　*Flor.* Hesperus, thou art mad.

*Hesp.* Better be mad than treacherous. Aye, 'twas
    well
To tear the letters; there might be a husband;
No, he shall be no more.
    *Flor.*                 But listen to me,
These lips that thou hast kissed,—
    *Hesp.*              I, and a thousand,
Men, boys, and monsters.
    *Flor.*            And these arms thou callest
Beloved and fair—
    *Hesp.*           And fickle and adulterous.
Enough of woman: boy, your paramour
Is troublesome, sirrah, milk-blooded imp,
Raise her; she loves your silken limbs; I give you
All that is mine of her.
    *Flor.*            Oh! save me, dearest.
    *Hesp.* She speaks to you, sir. I beseech you
    both,
Go on; don't heed me: oh, I joy to see
Your love-tricks.
    *Flor.*         By the solemn spousal tie,
I charge you, hear me.
    *Hesp.*           Lady, I will tell you,
Though it is needless, what I meant to say,
And leave you then for ever. You remember
A loving dupe you entertained some while,
One Hesperus, you must; oh! that you ever
Forgot him. Well, I will be brief. He gave you,
And bade you keep it as you would his love,
A little bird, a sweet red-bosomed creature,
To toy with in his absence: (then he knew not
You had another playmate for your chamber.)
This bird, it was a creature that I loved,

Yet it did not deceive me; I have thought
There was a spirit in it—never mind;
I dreamed I spoke to one, who valued me
And my poor feelings.   Unto you I gave it,
And you have lost it; in my way I passed
Its silent wicker house.   Now I have spoken,
Perhaps was tedious: but I'm still so foolish,
That I will say, good-bye.

 *Flor.*      Oh stay, my love.

 *Hesp.* He will, the lovely cub.

 *Flor.*      Thee, thee I mean.

 *Hesp.* I am no lover, I.   Madam, we're
  strangers;
And yet I knew some while ago a form
Like thine, as fair, as delicate.   Oh heaven!
To think of it.   But she was innocent,
Innocent, innocent.

 *Flor.*    The angels know
I am as spotless.

 *Hesp.*   Go to them; I'm not one;
Perhaps this pap-faced chit may be.   Nay, girl,
Wet not thy cheeks: I've seen a player weep.
I will not go, for if I do, the flock
Of her warm suitors will be toying here;
Yet I'll not stay; for she will melt and pray
Till I'm a fool again.   Strain not your lungs
With laughter when I'm gone.   Oh woman,
  woman.       [*Exit.*

 *Flor.* Poor boy, thou hast undone me: lead
  me in.        [*Exeunt.*

## SCENE III.

*An apartment in Orlando's palace.*

*Enter* HESPERUS.

*Hesp.* Oh thou sad self, thou wretched half of
    Hesperus,
Thou'rt lost indeed, there's nought of life about
    thee,
But the one thought, that thou hast saved a father.
Now I do think that if I meet a goodness
In woman's shape, a fair one I'd not ask,
But something that would soothe and comfort
    me,
I could almost love her.

*Enter* ORLANDO *and* OLIVIA.

*Orl.* My brother Hesperus, our poor home is
    honoured
By thy loved father's presence and thine own.
Here is a living welcome, prithee know her ;
Olivia.
    *Hesp.* Blessedness, you should have said.
A music waits upon her every step,
That my heart leaps to.
    *Oliv.*            Courtly, sir, and kind.
    *Hesp.* And fond I would have made it.    Oh
    fair lady,
A smile of thine will give me health again.

*Orl.* Sister, thou needst no witness to these
    blushes.
School her, sir, in the arts of compliment,
You'll find her an apt learner.                [*Exit.*

    *Oliv.* Had I a right to pray to you, I would.

    *Hesp.* Pray, lady? Didst thou ever see the
        goddess
Step from her dignity of stone, or leave
The hallowed picture in its tinted stole,
And crouch unto her suppliant? Oh no;
If there is aught so poor a thing as I
Can please you with, command it and you bless me.

    *Oliv.* Try, I beseech thee, try not to detest,
Not utterly to detest a silly girl,
Whose only merit is that she'd be thine.

    *Hesp.* Hate thee, thou virtue?

    *Oliv.* Well, if it must be,
Play the deceiver for a little while;
Don't tell me so.

    *Hesp.*        By Truth's white name I'll tell thee,
Olivia, there was once an idle thought
That aped affection in my heart; nay, nay,
Not in my heart; it was a dream or so;
A dream within a dream; a pale, dim warmth;
But thou hast dawned like summer on my soul,
Or like a new existence.

    *Oliv.*                  'Twere delightful,
If credible; but you are all too gallant.

    *Hesp.* I knew it must be so: you'll not believe
        me,
But doubt and say 'tis sudden. Do not minute
The movements of the soul, for some there are,
Of pinion unimpeded, thrice word-swift,

Outsoar the sluggish flesh ; and these, Olivia,
Anticipating their death-given powers, can grasp
A century of feeling and of thought ;
Outlive the old world's age, and be at once
In the present, past, and future ; while the body
Lives half a pulse's stroke.   To see and love
    thee
Was but one soul's step.

   *Oliv.*          Then thou canst endure me ;
Thou dost not hate the forward maid ?  My prayer
Through many a year has been for that one word ;
And I have kept the precious thought of thee,
Hidden almost from myself.   But I'll not speak,
For I have told too much, too childishly.

   *Hesp.* Dear, I could weep, but that my brain
    is dry,
To think upon thee.   *Me*—'Twere well to court
The yellow pestilence, or woo the lightning
Unto thy bosom ; but to hold me dear—
It is a crime of hell ; forget you thought it.

   *Oliv.* 'Tis sweeter than a virtue, I must love
    thee.

   *Hesp.* And love me truly?

   *Oliv.*              Heaven grant me life
To prove it.

   *Hesp.* Then thou shalt be mine own ; but not
    till death :
We'll let this life burn out, no matter how ;
Though every sand be moistened with our tears,
And every day be rain-wet in our eyes ;
Though thou shouldst wed some hateful avarice,
And I grow hoary with a daubed deceit,
A smiling treachery in woman's form,

Sad to the soul, heart-cankered and forlorn ;
No matter, all no matter.
Though madness rule our thoughts, despair our
   hearts,
And misery live with us, and misery talk,
Our guest all day, our bed-fellow all night ;
No matter, all no matter.
For when our souls are born then will we wed ;
Our dust shall mix and grow into one stalk,
Our breaths shall make one perfume in one bud,
Our blushes meet eace other in a rose,
Our sweeter voices swell some sky-bird's throat
With the same warbling, dwell in some soft pipe,
Or bubble up along some sainted spring's
Musical course, and in the mountain trees
Slumber our deeper tones, by tempests waked :
We will be music, spring, and all fair things,
The while our spirits make a sweeter union
Than melody and perfume in the air.
Wait then, if thou dost love me.
  *Oliv.*       Be it so ;
You'll let me pray for death, if it will bring
Such joys as these ? Though once I thought to live
A happy bride ; but I must learn new feelings.
  *Hesp.* New feelings ! Aye to watch the lagging
   clock,
And bless each moment as it parts from thee,
To court the blighting grasp of tardy age,
And search thy forehead for a silver tress
As for a most prized jewel.
  *Oliv.*      I cannot think
Of that cold bed diseases make for us,
That earthy sleep : oh ! 'tis a dreadful thing.

*Hesp.* The very air,
I thank it, (the same wild and busy air,
That numbers every syllable I speak,
In the same instant my lips shape its sound,
With the first lisps of him, who died before
The world began its story;) steals away
A little from my being;
And at each slightest tremour of a leaf
My hearse moves one step nearer.   Joy, my love!
We're nearer to our bridal sheets of lead
Than when your brother left us here just now,
By twenty minutes' talk.
    *Oliv.*               It is not good
Thus to spurn life, the precious gift of heaven,
And watch the coming light of dissolution
With such a desperate hope.   Can we not love
In secret, and be happy in our thoughts,
Till in devotion's train, th' appointed hour
Lead us, with solemnly rejoicing hearts,
Unto our blessed end?
    *Hesp.*             End! thou sayest.
And do those cherries ripen for the worms,
Those blue enchantments beam to light the tomb?
Was that articulate harmony, (Love uses
Because he seems both Love and Innocence
When he sings to it,) that summer of sweet breath,
Created but to perish and so make
The dead's home loveliest?
    *Oliv.* But what's to live without my Hesperus?
A life of dying.   'Tis to die each moment
In every several sense.   To look despair,
Feel, taste, breathe, eat, be conscious of despair.
No, I'll be nothing rather.

*Hesp.*                    Nothing but mine !
Thou flower of love, I'll wear thee in my bosom ;
With thee the wrath of man will be no wrath,
Conscience and agony will smile like pleasure,
And sad remembrance lose its gloomy self
In rapturous expectation.
    *Oliv.*                    Let me look on thee ;
Pray pardon me, mine eyes are very fools.
    *Hesp.* Jewels of pity, azure stars of beauty
Which lost affection steers by ; could I think
To dim your light with sorrow ?   Pardon me,
And I will serve you ever.   Sweet, go in ;
Somewhat I have to think on.        [*Exit* OLIVIA.
                   Floribel,
I would not have thee cross my path to-night ;
There is an indistinct dread purpose forming,
Something, whose depth of wickedness appears
Hideous, incalculable, but inevitable ;
Now it draws nearer, and I do not shudder ;
Avaunt ! haunt me no more ; I dread it not,
But almost—hence !   I must not be alone.
                      [*Exit.*


## SCENE IV.

*A tapestried chamber in the same.*

HESPERUS *discovered in a disturbed slumber.*

    *Hesp.* (*starting from his couch*).  Who speaks ?
Who whispers there ?  A light ! a light !

I'll search the room, something hath called me
    thrice,
With a low muttering voice of toadish hisses,
And thrice I slept again.   But still it came
Nearer and nearer, plucked my mantle from me,
And made mine heart an ear, in which it poured
Its loathed enticing courtship.   Ho ! a light.


      *Enter* Attendant *with a torch.*

Thou drowsy snail, thy footsteps are asleep,
Hold up the torch.
   *Attend.*          My lord, you are disturbed.
Have you seen aught ?
   *Hesp.*            I lay upon my bed,
And something in the air, out-jetting night,
Converting feeling to intenser vision,
Featured its ghastly self upon my soul
Deeper than sight.
   *Attend.*         This is Delusion surely ;
She's busy with men's thoughts at all night
    hours,
And to the waking subtle apprehension
The darkling chamber's still and sleepy air
Hath breath and motion oft.
    *Hesp.*  Lift up the hangings, mark the doors, the
    corners ;
Seest nothing yet ?   No face of fiendlike mirth,
More frightful than the fixed and doggish grin
Of a dead madman ?
   *Attend.*         Nought I see, my lord,
Save the long, varied crowd of warlike shapes
Set in the stitched picture.

*Hesp.*                    Heard ye then?
There was a sound, as though some marble tongue
Moved on its rusty hinge, syllabling harshly
The hoarse death-rattle into speech.
   *Attend.* The wind is high, and through the
     silent rooms
Murmurs his burthen, to an heedless ear
Almost articulate.
   *Hesp.*            Thou sleepest, fool;
A voice has been at my bedside to-night,
Its breath is burning on my forehead still,
Still o'er my brain its accents, wildly sweet,
Hover and fall.   Away and dream again:
I'll watch myself.
     [*He takes the torch and turns to the hangings.*
                  [*Exit* Attendant.
         Aye, these are living colours,
Those cheeks have worn their youth these hundred
     years,
Those flowers are verdant in their worsted spring
And blooming still;
While she, whose needle limned so cunningly,
Sleeps and dreams not.   It is a goodly state,
And there is one I wish had ta'en her bed
In the stone dormitory.
              (Blindfold moth,
Thou shalt not burn thy life; there, I have saved
     thee;
If thou art grateful, mingle with the air
That feeds the lips of her I thought of once,
Choak her, moth, choak her.   I could be content
If she were safe in heaven.)
             Yon stout dagger

Is fairly fashioned for a blade of stitches,
And shines, methinks, most grimly; well, thou ˉ
    art
An useful tool sometimes, thy tooth works quickly,
And, if thou gnawest a secret from the heart,
Thou tellest it not again : ha ! the feigned steel
Doth blush and steam.    There is a snuff of blood.
            [*Grasps his dagger convulsively.*
Who placed this iron aspic in my hand?
Speak ! who is at my ear?
            [*He turns, and addresses his shadow.*
                    I know thee now,
I know the hideous laughter of thy face.
'Tis Malice' eldest imp, the heir of hell,
Red-handed Murther.    Slow it whispers me,
Coaxingly with its serpent voice.    Well sung,
Syren of Acheron !
                I'll not look on thee;
Why does thy frantic weapon dig the air
With such most frightful vehemence?    Back, back,
Tell the dark grave I will not give it food.
Back to thy home of night.    What ! playest thou
    still?
Then thus I banish thee.    Out, treacherous torch,
Sure thou wert kindled in infernal floods,
Or thy bright eye would blind at sights like this.
            [*Dashes the torch on the ground.*
Tempt me no more ; I tell thee, Floribel
Shall never bleed.    I pray thee, guilty word,
Tempt me no more.
            [*Wraps himself in his mantle.*
                I'm deaf, my ears are safe,
I do not hear thee woo me to the deed ;

I.                                      K

Thou tellest to one without auricular sense
Olivia's beauties and that bad one's faults.
Oh! bring me thoughts of pity. Come, come,
    come,
Or I am lost.

                    Bad goblin, must I fly thee? [*Exit.*


## Scene V.

### *A hall in the same.*

Lord Ernest, Orlando, Claudio, Olivia.

*L. Ern.* Saw ye my son?
.*Oliv.*                 Some hours ago we parted,
And he was strange, though gentle, in his talk.
*Orl.* I passed him in the garden, just at twilight;
He stood with eyes wide open, but their sense
Dreamed, in dumb parley with some fancied thing;
For his lips moved, and he did walk and gaze,
Now frown most mournfully, now smile most madly,
And weep, and laugh, groan deep and gnash his
        teeth,
And now stand still with such a countenance,
As does the marble sorrow o'er a tomb.
At last he tore his feet, as they were roots,
Up from the earth, and sighed like one o'ercome;
Then, with his fingers thrust upon his eyes
And dashed unclosed away, he seemed to snatch
Some loathly object out of them, and leapt
Into the thicket's gloom.
    *L. Ern.*        .        Who saw him since?

*Clau.* In most distempered wildness he hath left
His chamber now.

    *L. Ern.*          Go seek him, every one,
I do beseech you ; 'tis a fearful period,
I know too truly.   On his nurse's breast,
Some twenty years ago, he lay and mused
Upon her singing and bright merry lips ;
A viewless bolt dropped on her, and she died
Most hideously ; close in the infant's face
Looked all the horrors of her bursting eyes ;
And, as the months bring round that black remem-
      brance,
His brain unsettles, bloody thoughts oppress
And call him from his bed.   Search all the darkness,
Each one a several way ; dear daughter, in.

                        [*Exeunt.*

## SCENE VI.

*A suicide's grave.*

ORLANDO *and* CLAUDIO.

    *Clau.* There is a plague in this night's breath,
      Orlando,
The dews fall black and blistering from yon cloud
Anchored above us ; dost thou mark how all
The smokes of heaven avoid it and crowd on
Far from its fatal darkness ?  Some men say
That the great king of evil sends his spirits
In such a winged car, to stir ill minds
Up to an act of death.

    *Orl.*             We may not think so,

For there's a fascination in bad deeds,
Oft pondered o'er, that draws us to endure them,
And then commit.   Beware of thine own soul :
'Tis but one devil ever tempts a man,
And his name's *Self.*   Know'st thou these rankling
    hemlocks?
  *Clau.* I've seen the ugsome reptiles battening on
    them,
While healthy creatures sicken at the sight.
  *Orl.* Five months ago they were an human heart,
Beating in Hugo's breast.   A parricide
Here sleeps, self-slaughtered.   'Twas a thing of
    grace,
In his early infancy; I've known him oft
Outstep his pathway, that he might not crush
The least small reptile.   But there is a time
When goodness sleeps; it came, and vice was
    grafted
On his young thoughts, and grew, and flourished
    there :
Envenomed passions clustered round that prop ;
A double fruit they bore ; a double fruit of death.
  *Clau.* Enough, Orlando,
The imps of darkness listen, while we tell
A dead man's crimes.   Even now I heard a stir,
As if the buried turned them in their shrouds
For mere unquiet.   Home, it is the time
When the hoarse fowl, the carrier-bird of woe,
Brings fevers from the moon, and maddening
    dreams ;
The hour's unholy, and who hath not sent
After the parted sun his orisons,
Falls 'neath the sway of evil.        [*Exeunt.*

*Enter* HESPERUS.

*Hesp.* Hail, shrine of blood, in double shadows
    veiled,
Where the Tartarian blossoms shed their poison
And load the air with wicked impulses ;
Hail, leafless shade, hallowed to sacrilege,
Altar of death ! Where is thy deity?
With him I come to covenant, and thou,
Dark power, that sittest in the chair of night,
Searching the clouds for tempests with thy brand,
Proxy of Hades ; list and be my witness,
And bid your phantoms all, (the while I speak
What, if they but repeat in sleeping ears,
Will strike the hearer dead, and mad his soul ;)
Spread wide and black and thick their cloudy
    wings,
Lest the appalled sky do pale to-day.
Eternal people of the lower world,
Ye citizens of Hades' capitol,
That by the rivers of remorseful tears
Sit and despair for ever ;
Ye negro brothers of the deadly winds,
Ye elder souls of night, ye mighty sins,
Sceptred damnations, how may man invoke
Your darkling glories? Teach my eager soul
Fit language for your ears. Ye that have power
O'er births and swoons and deaths, the soul's
    attendants,
(Wont to convey her from her human home
Beyond existence, to the past or future,
To lead her through the starry-blossomed meads,
Where the young hours of morning by the lark

With earthly airs are nourished, through the groves
Of silent gloom, beneath whose breathless shades
The thousand children of Calamity
Play murtherously with men's hearts :) Oh pause,
Your universal occupations leave,
Lay down awhile the infant miseries,
That, to the empty and untenanted clay,
Ye carry from the country of the unborn ;
And grant the summoned soul one moment
        more
To linger on the threshold of its flesh ;
For I would task you.

                Bear this breath of mine,
This inner Hesperus away, and bring
Another guest to its deserted home ;
The mind of him whose dust is on my feet,
And let his daring spirit inhabit there
But for a passing day.

                   'Tis here.   A wind
Is rushing through my veins, and I become
As a running water.
I see a shadowy image of myself,
Yet not my perfect self, a brother self,
That steps into my bosom.   Am I born
Newly, or newly dead ?   I'll think a little.
Have I e'er lived before, or thought or acted ?
Why no ; it was the morning doze of being,
I slept content with dreams ; but now I wake
And find it noon, a time for stirring deeds.
Yes, this is life that trembles in my veins,
Yes, this is courage warms my heart's full tide :
Hesperus is a man, a demon-man,
And there's a thing he lives for, shall amaze

The emulous bad powers.
                              Lead me on,
Mysterious guide, companion wickedness ;
Olivia calls me forward, and, to reach her,
What if we tread upon a world of hearts ?
Come, ye ill blasts, ye killing visitants
Of sleeping men, wild creatures of the air,
We'll walk together ; come, ye beauteous snakes,
Ye lovely fanged monsters of the woods,
We'll grovel in the dust and ye shall hiss
Your tunes of murder to me.
                              [*An ignis fatuus rises.*
                         Lo, she's here
To light our sports, the Hebe of the dead,
Alecto, 'mid her nest of living hair
Bearing a star of Tartarus.   Lead on.      [*Exit.*


# ACT III.

## SCENE I.

*An apartment in Orlando's palace.*

HESPERUS *seated.*  Attendants.  *Enter to them*
CLAUDIO.

*Clau.* The bridegroom's here ?
*Attend.*                 Yonder he sits, my lord,
And since the morn's first hour, without the motion
Even of a nerve, as he were growing marble,

Has sat and watched : the sun blazed in at noon
With light enough to blind an eagle's ken ;
He felt it not, although his eyeballs glared
Horribly bright : I spoke ; he heard me not ;
And, when I shook his arm, slept on in thought :
I pray you try him.
    *Clau.*          Sir, good Hesperus,
I wait at your desire ; we are to end
Our match at tennis. Will you walk with me ?
    *Attend.* Your voice is weak as silence to his
       sense.

*Enter* ORLANDO.

    *Orl.* My brother, you must join us at the
       banquet ;
We wait your coming long ; how's this ?
    *Attend.*            My lord,
Like trance has held him since the dawn of day ;
He has looked down upon yon wood since then,
Speechless and still.

*Enter* LORD ERNEST.

    *L. Ern.*      Now health and good be here,
For I have missed my son the livelong day.
Why, what an idle loiterer thou art ;
By this, your vacant sight must ache with gazing
Upon that view.   Arise ; I'd have you with me,
To fix upon some posy for the ring
You wed your love with.   Death !   Some fearful
       change
Is here.   Speak ; speak and tell me if he lives.
    *Attend.* He does, my lord, if breathing is to live,
But in all else is like the coffined dead ;

Motion and speech he lacks.

*L. Ern.*                    O heavens! Orlando,
Tell me 'tis false.

*Orl.*              I would 'twere in my power,
But it doth seem too true.

*L. Ern.*                  Ride like the wind,
Fetch him the aid of medicine.   See you not
Some vision has come to him in the night,
And stolen his eyes and ears and tongue away?

*Enter* OLIVIA.

Oh, you are come in time to see him die;
Look, look, Olivia, look; he knows us not;
My son, if thou dost hear me, speak one word,
And I will bless thee.

*Orl.*                He is dumb indeed.

*Oliv.* Let me come near him.  Dearest Hesperus,
If thou behold'st these poor unbeauteous cheeks,
Which first thy flattering kindness taught to blush;
Or if thou hearest a voice, that's only sweet
When it says Hesperus; oh gentle love,
Speak any thing, even that thou hatest Olivia,
And I will thank thee for't: or, if some horror
Has frozen up the fountain of thy words,
Give but a sign.

*Clau.*              Lady, alas, 'tis vain.

*Oliv.* (*kneeling*).  Nay, he shall speak, or I will
      never move,
But thus turn earth beseeching his dull hand,
And let the grass grow over me.   I'll hold
A kind of converse with my raining eyes,
For if he sees not, nor doth hear, he'll know
The gentle feel of his Olivia's tears.

*Clau.*                     Sweet sir, look on her.
*Orl.* Brother !
*Oliv.*              Husband !
*L. Ern.*                       Son !
Kind heaven, let him hear, though death should
      call him.              [*Pause, a clock strikes.*
*Hesp.*   The hour is come.                 [*Exit.*


## SCENE II.

*A room in Mordred's cottage.*

### FLORIBEL *alone.*

*Flor.*   And must I wake again ?  Oh come to me,
Thou that with dew-cold fingers softly closest
The wearied eye ; thou sweet, thou gentle power,
Soother of woe, sole friend of the oppressed,
I long to lay me on thy peaceful breast.
But once I saw thee, beautiful as moonlight,
Upon a baby's lips, and thou didst kiss them,
Lingering and oft,
(As a wild bee doth kiss a rifled flower,
And clips its waist, and drops a little tear,
Remorsefully enamoured of his prey ;)
Come so to me, sweet death, and I will wreath
      thee
An amorous chaplet for thy paly brows ;
And, on an odoured bank of wan white buds,
In thy fair arms
I'll lie, and taste thy cool delicious breath,
And sleep, and sleep, and sleep.

*Enter* LENORA.

        O here, good mother,
We'll talk together.
 *Len.*     What ; of Hesperus?
Methinks he has grown cold.
 *Flor.*      Oh no ; he is
More full of courtship than he ever was ;
Don't think him cold, dear mother, or I may :
I'm sure he loves me still ; I'll go to him,
'Tis nigh the appointed hour.
 *Len.* My child, it is a chill and gloomy evening,
So go not out. Thy Hesperus will come,
And thou wilt live on every word of his
Till thine eyes sparkle. What means this despond-
   ence ?
 *Flor.* Dear mother, I will strive to be at ease,
If you desire ; but melancholy thoughts
Are poor dissemblers. How I wish we owned
The wealth we've lost.
 *Len.*     Why girl, I never heard
One such regret escape your lips before ;
Has not your Hesperus enough?
 *Flor.*      Too much ;
If he were even poorer than ourselves,
I'd almost love him better. For, methinks,
It seemed a covetous spirit urged me on,
Craving to be received his bride. I hope
He did not think so ; if he does, I'll tell him
I will not share his wealth, but dwell with you.
O that he'd come ! How each dull moment drags
Its lazy wing along when he is absent.

When was he here?

   *Len.*             Last night.

   *Flor.* Last night? Now pr'ythee
Don't jeer me so, I'm sure, not many days;
But all is night when he's not here to light me,
So let it be last night; although that night
Had days for hours, yet in Love's book and
      mine
'Tis but an empty cypher, a black round.
Oh, I've not lived, I've not been Floribel
Since the last mellow echo of his voice
Lent the air music; is't not a sweet voice?
What can you liken to it?

   *Len.*           Pan's honeycomb
Of many vocal cells.

   *Flor.*          How dull you are;
There's nought beneath the thunder-choir so grand;
The wood-birds and the waterfalls but mock him.
He said, dear mother, I should be his countess;
To-day he'd come to fetch me, but with day
I've laid my expectation in its grave.
Dost think he will deceive me? Silly girl,
Querulous ingrate, why do I torment me?
Sweet mother, comfort.

   *Len.*         Be you sure he'll come
With his whole princely train of friends and kin-
      dred,
And he will lift thee to his gorgeous car,
And place thee at his side, a happy wife.

   *Flor.* Fie! you cajole me, like a sulky child,
With gilded cars; but oh! I wish 'twere here.
How gloomily the clouds look, and the wind
Rattles among the brown leaves dolefully;

He will be very chill, heap up the fire.
Hush ! hark ! What's that ?
    *Len.*                      Only your dear father
Heavily breathing in his sleep ; he'll wake
With his sad smile upon his patient face,
Looking so dear in sickness.
    *Flor.*                  But 'twill cure him,
When he knows all and sees my bridegroom with
    me,
I know it will : and there's the horse's step,
I'll just run out, it is not cold at all.—
    *Len.*                     Go, my love,
But you must come to ask your father's blessing,
And bring your Hesperus with you.
    *Flor.*                     That I will.
                               [*Exeunt.*


## SCENE III.

### *A wood.*

#### *Enter* HUBERT *and a* Huntsman.

    *Hub.* No answer to our shouts but mocking
    echo ?
Where are our fellow huntsmen ? Why, they
    vanished
Like mist before the sun, and left us here
Lost in the briary mazes.
    *Hunts.*                Shame on the rogues
For this their treatment. But look upwards,
    Hubert,
See what a mighty storm hangs right above us.

*Hub.* The day is in its shroud while yet an
    infant ;
And Night with giant strides stalks o'er the world,
Like a swart Cyclops, on its hideous front
One round, red, thunder-swollen eye ablaze.
    *Hunts.* Now mercy save the peril-stricken man,
Who 'mongst his shattered canvas sits aghast
On the last sinking plank alone, and sees
The congregated monsters of the deep
For his dead messmates warring all, save one
That leers upon him with a ravenous gaze,
And whets its iron tusks just at his feet :
Yet little heeds his wide and tearless eye
That, or the thunder of the mountain flood
Which Destiny commissions with his doom ;
Where the wild waters rush against the sky,
Far o'er the desolate plain, his star of hope
In mockery gleams, while death is at his side.
                     [*Lightning.*
    *Hub.* That flash hath rent the heavens; this
    way for shelter.
    *Hunts.* Some steps above there stands a noble
    oak,
That from the sun roofs ever-during night
With its thickwoven firmament of leaves:
Thither betake we.            [*Exeunt.*

*Enter* FLORIBEL.

    *Flor.* Hence did I seem to hear a human voice,
Yet there is nought, save a low moaning sound,
As if the spirits of the earth and air
Were holding sad and ominous discourse.
And much I fear me I have lost my path ;

Oh how these brambles tear; here 'twixt the willows;
Ha! something stirs; my silly prattling nurse
Says that fierce shaggy wolves inhabit here,
And 'tis in sooth a dread and lonely place;
There, there again; a rustling in the leaves.

*Enter* HESPERUS.

'Tis he at last; why dost thou turn away
And lock thy bosom from my first embrace?
I am so tired and frightened; but thou'rt here;
I knew thou wouldst be faithful to thy promise,
And claim me openly. Speak, let me hear thy voice,
Tell me the joyful news.

*Hesp.*                    Aye, I am come
In all my solemn pomp; Darkness and Fear,
And the great Tempest in his midnight car,
The sword of lightning girt across his thigh,
And the whole dæmon brood of night, blind Fog
And withering Blight, all these are my retainers;
How: not one smile for all this bravery?
What think you of my minstrels, the hoarse winds,
Thunder, and tuneful Discord? Hark, they play.
Well piped, methinks; somewhat too rough,
        perhaps.

*Flor.* I know you practise on my silliness,
Else I might well be scared. But leave this mirth,
Or I must weep.

*Hesp.*                  'Twill serve to fill the goblets
For our carousal; but we loiter here,
The bridemaids are without, well-picked thou'lt say,
Wan ghosts of woe-begone, self-slaughtered damsels
In their best winding sheets; start not, I bid them
        wipe

Their gory bosoms; they'll look wondrous comely;
Our link-boy, Will o' the Wisp, is waiting too
To light us to our grave——bridal I mean.

   *Flor.* Ha! how my veins are chilled—why,
      Hesperus!

   *Hesp.* What hero of thy dreams art calling,
      girl?
Look in my face—Is't mortal? Dost thou think
The voice that calls thee is not of a mouth
Long choaked with dust? What, though I have
      assumed
This garb of flesh, and with it the affections,
The thoughts of weakness and mortality?
'Twas but for thee; and now thou art my bride;
Lift up thine eyes and smile—the bride of Death.

   *Flor.* Hold, hold. My thoughts are wildered.
      Is my fancy
The churlish framer of these fearful words,
Or do I live indeed to such a fate?
Oh! no, I recollect; I have not waked
Since Hesperus left me in the twilight bower.

   *Hesp.* Come, we'll to our chamber,
The cypress shade hangs o'er our stony couch,
A goodly canopy; be mad and merry;
There'll be a jovial feast among the worms.
Fiends, strew your fiercest fire about my heart, [*aside.*
Or she will melt it.

   *Flor.*           Oh, that look of fury!
What's this about my eyes? ah! deadly night,
No light, no hope, no help.

   *Hesp.*         What! Darest thou tremble
Under thy husband's arm, darest think of fear?
Dost dread me, me?

*Flor.*  I know not what to dread,
Nor what to hope ; all's horrible and doubtful ;
And coldness creeps—
*Hesp.*  She swoons, poor girl, she swoons.
And, treacherous dæmons, ye've allowed a drop
To linger in my eyes.  Out, out for ever.
I'm fierce again.  Now shall I slay the victim
As she lies senseless ? ah ! she wakes ; cheer up,
'Twas but a jest.
*Flor.*  A dread and cruel one ;
But I'll forgive you, if you will be kind ;
And yet 'twas frightful.
*Hesp.*  Why, 'twere most unseemly
For one marked for the grave to laugh too loud.
*Flor.* Alas ! he raves again.  Sweetest, what
mean you
By these strange words?
*Hesp.*  What mean I ?  Death and murder,
Darkness and misery.  To thy prayers and shrift ;
Earth gives thee back ; thy God hath sent me for
thee ;
Repent and die.
*Flor.*  Oh, if thou willest it, love,
If thou but speak it with thy natural voice,
And smile upon me ; I'll not think it pain,
But cheerfully I'll seek me out a grave,
And sleep as sweetly as on Hesperus' breast.
He will not smile, he will not listen to me.
Why dost thou thrust thy fingers in thy bosom ?
Oh search it, search it ; see if there remain
One little remnant of thy former love,
To dry my tears with.
*Hesp.*  Well, speak on ; and then,

I.  L

When thou hast done thy tale, I will but kill thee.
Come tell me all my vows, how they are broken,
Say that my love was feigned, and black deceit ;
Pour out thy bitterest, till untamed wrath
Melt all his chains off with his fiery breath,
And rush a-hungering out.

    *Flor.*                  O piteous heavens !
I see it now, some wild and poisonous creature
Hath wounded him, and with contagious fang
Planted this fury in his veins.   He hides
The mangled fingers ; dearest, trust them to me,
I'll suck the madness out of every pore,
So as I drink it boiling from thy wound
Death will be pleasant.   Let me have the hand,
And I will treat it like another heart.

    *Hesp.*                     Here 'tis then ;
                                [*Stabs her.*

Shall I thrust deeper yet ?

    *Flor.*             Quite through my soul,—
That all my senses, deadened at the blow,
May never know the giver.   Oh, my love,
Some spirit in thy sleep hath stolen thy body
And filled it to the brim with cruelty.
Farewell ; and may no busy deathful tongue
Whisper this horror in thy waking ears,
Lest some dread desperate sorrow urge thy soul
To deeds of wickedness.   Whose kiss is that ?
His lips are ice.   Oh my loved Hesperus,
Help !                          [*Dies.*

    *Hesp.* What a shriek was that ; it flew to heaven,
And hymning angels took it for their own.
Dead art thou, Floribel ; fair, painted earth,
And no warm breath shall ever more disport

Between those rubious lips : no, they have quaffed
Life to the dregs, and found death at the bottom,
The sugar of the draught.  All cold and still ;
Her very tresses stiffen in the air.
Look, what a face : had our first mother worn
But half such beauty, when the serpent came,
His heart, all malice, would have turned to love.
No hand but this, which I do think was once
Cain, the arch-murtherer's, could have acted it.
And I must hide these sweets, not in my bosom ;
In the foul earth.   She shudders at my grasp ;
Just so she laid her head across my bosom
When first—oh villain ! which way lies the grave ?
                                        [*Exit.*

*Enter* HUBERT *and a* Huntsman.

*Hub.*  It is a fearful and tempestuous time :
The concave firmament, the angel's bridge
O'er the world's day and night, is visibly
Bowed down and bent beneath its load of thunder ;
And through the fiery fissures of the clouds
Glistens the warfare of armed elements,
Bellowing defiance in earth's stunned ear,
And setting midnight on the throne of day.
    *Hunts.*  The roar has ceased ; the hush of inter-
        calm
'Numbs with its leaden finger Echo's lips,
And angry spirits in mid havoc pause,
Premeditating ruin in their silence.
    *Hub.*  Hard by should stand a lone and tattered
        shed,
Where some tired woodsman may by chance be
    stretched,

Watching his scanty food among the coals;
There may we chafe our drenched and chilly limbs.

   *Hunts.* The forest has more tenants than I knew:
Look underneath this branch; seest thou not yonder,
Amongst the brushwood and the briary weeds,
A man at work?

   *Hub.*      My life upon't some miser,
Who in the secret hour creeps to his hoard,
And, kneeling at the altar of his love,
Worships that yellow devil, gold.

   *Hunts.*         'Tis buried;
And now he stamps the sod down, that no light
May spy his mistress; with what a doleful look
He marks its grave, and backward walks away,
As if he left his all of sight behind.

   *Hub.* Let us steal towards it; I would have a
      peep
Upon this hidden jewel.        [*Exeunt.*

### *Enter* HESPERUS.

   *Hesp.* Shall I turn back and try to thrust my soul
In at her lips, and so re-animate
The beauteous casket while this body dies?
I cannot :—not the universe of breath
Could give those little lips their life again.
I've huddled her into the wormy earth,
And left the guilty dagger at her side.
Dead Innocence! and must unkindly thistles,
And rank thick hemlock, force their bristling roots
Into thy lovely breast? Fool! Is't not done?
Why stand I tampering midst the listening winds?
My fears are lying traitors.   [*Bells at a distance.*
                  Wedding bells,

Thanks for your merry voices; ye have waked
A sudden hurry round about my heart,
I'll think it joy.   Now for my second bride. [*Exit.*


### SCENE IV.

*A saloon in Orlando's palace.*

OLIVIA, VIOLETTA, Nurse, *and* Attendants.

*Oliv.* You keep me long : am I not yet attired ?
Have ye not tricked me out enough ?   In faith,
I am so vain to think I need no more.
  *Attend.* One moment, madam ;
This little necklace, like the marriage yoke
Pleasantly binding, I must clasp around you.
  *Oliv.* A pretty toy, and prettily disposed ;
I have, I know not why, this livelong day
Wept drops enough to bead a thousand such.
Where's Violetta ?   Come, look up, my girl,
Make thine eyes sparkle ; mine are very moist.
  *Viol.* Shake off this sadness, lady, 'tis not meet
At such a moment ; think upon your bridegroom,
How his affections seek thee.
  *Oliv.*                              Gentle maid,
I'll not be sad ; yet, little Violet,
How long I've worn thy beauty next my heart,
Aye, in my very thoughts, where thou hast shed
Perpetual summer : how long shared thy being :
Like two leaves of a bud, we've grown together,
And needs must bleed at parting.
  *Viol.*                              No, not so ;
I am thy handmaid still ; and when your lord

Is absent, as he will be, at the tourney,
The court, or camp, we'll drive the long hours on
With prattle as of old.

    *Oliv.*              Thanks, I'll be cheerful;
But joy's a plant the showers of many sorrows
Must water, ere it bloom.  Good nurse, your
    pardon,
You've known me for a froward child before.

    *Nurse.*  Now, on the scanty remnant of my life,
Grief's an ill wedding garment; if you'd put
One of your rosy smiles on, what a grace
You'd look and be.   Why, all these ohs and sobs
Are more like funeral noises.

    *Oliv.*            'Troth they are,
And 'tis the funeral of that Olivia
You nursed and knew; an hour and she's no more,
No more the mistress of her own resolves,
The free partaker of earth's airs and pleasures;
My very love, the poorest gift I have,
(Which, light as 'tis, I thought you all did prize,)
Is not my own.   We must be strangers, girls;
Give me your hands and wishes.

    *Nurse.*          There is one,
Old now, and withered, truly we might call it
Yours, and not mine; oft has it brought you food,
Led you, and served you; yet in gladness parts
To make way for a younger and a worthier.

    *Oliv.*  My kind old nurse; nay, now you are
    forgetting
Your words of cheer; this hand shall never want
Aid while I live, your service will be needful;
My house would seem a strange and dismal place
Without your pleasant looks.

*Nurse.*                          Well, my dear child,
I hope you'll give my arms a new Olivia ;
Blush not ; the old will talk.
    *Oliv.*                          Whose hand is this
I know not from my own ?  Young Violet's ?
My beauteous innocence, you must be with me
Oft, as you said : Go to, my nurse forbids
Our weeping.
    *Viol.*          Don't chide me then, Olivia,
I'm a sad fool, but do not chide.
    *Oliv.*                          A gem
For Friendship's crown, each drop.  My loving
      maids,
To each a farewell that I cannot speak ;
All have my heart, and well can read its meaning.
Henceforth I'll look upon my maiden years
As lovely pastoral pictures ; all of you
Shall smile again 'neath Memory's wizard pencil ;
The natural beauties that we've marked together
Will look you back again ; the books we've loved
Will talk to me of your sweet-worded praises,
The air of our old haunts whisper your voices ;
Trust me, I'll not forget you.
    *Attend.*                          Dearest lady,
May all the blessings that rain down from heaven
Upon the marriage-bed, descend on yours ;
May many children, innocent and fair,
With soft embracements throng about your knees,
Domestic pleasures ever turn your hour-glass,
And, when the long sleep falls upon your eyes,
Content and holy Peace, the twins of Eden,
Draw round the curtain 'twixt you and the world,
And watch beside you all the dreary night.

SCENE V.

*A room in Mordred's cottage.*

*Enter* LENORA *supporting* MORDRED.

*Mor.* Here let me rest, in my old oaken chair :
My limbs grow faint, and yet, kind, careful nurse,
Your smiles have chased away my pains.
 *Len.*         Dear husband,
A thousand thanks for those delightful words ;
They bid me hope again and warm my heart.
 *Mor.* It renovates the spirit thus to look,
With the clear eye of health and joyousness,
Upon the green creation. But I miss
A smile of hope, the copy of Lenora's,
That's wont to light my soul with its rich love ;
Where is my peach-cheeked girl, my Floribel?
 *Len.* She will be with us soon; before you
   woke,
She went to ramble underneath the boughs,
And feed her forest-birds ; each bower she knows
Of eglantine and hawthorn ; now the air
Is calm, she will return.
 *Mor.*       I hope she may ;
Yet who could injure such a holy thing?
The frenzied tempest's self, had it a will,
Would leave her path secure. My dear Lenora,
There is one thing I wish to see accomplished
Before I die.
 *Len.* What is it, love? And yet methinks 'twere fit
For me still to defer its execution,

And cheat you into living to that end.

 *Mor.* Long have I prayed to see her beauty
  growing
Under some worthy husband's firm protection.

 *Len.* What if she be already wedded?

 *Mor.*            No,
That cannot be, she would have told unto me
The first emotions of her infant love;
She never had a thought concealed from me,
Even her slightest. 'Tis impossible;
And yet you look in earnest; speak, and tell me
You only jest.

 *Len.*     I speak indeed the truth;
Perhaps I was imprudent not to tell you,
But you were very ill, and, such the match,
You could not disapprove: Young Hesperus—

 *Mor.* Lord Ernest's son!

 *Len.*       The same.

 *Mor.*         I'm satisfied,
My wish is all fulfilled. There's not a man
Beneath the sun more noble; but his father
Was wont to be a stern imperious lord,
A scorner of the poor.

 *Len.*      He did not know it.

 *Mor.* He knew it not! That was a sad omission,
Unworthy of a parent; we might rue it.

 *Len.* This night our daughter's bridegroom
Comes, as his own to claim her, and, ere this,
Doubtless has told the love-tale to his father.

 *Mor.* I wish him speedy, he shall find a welcome,
In the poor man's sole wealth, my hearty love.
Hark! There's a step.

 *Len.*      'Tis Hesperus'; I know it.

*Enter the* Huntsman.

*Mor.* Who comes, who is it?

*Len.*                    One, whose visage wears
The darkest sadness; such a man I'd choose
For the mute herald of disaster.

*Hunts.*                    Lady,
Would that my looks could mirror to your soul
The woe, each syllable of which in speaking
Tears through my heart. Alas! your lovely
        daughter—

*Len.* What? Speak I pray thee. Has she met
        with aught?

*Mor.* Bid me die, or my fears.

*Enter* HUBERT *with the body of* FLORIBEL.

*Hunts.* Here's all that's left
Of nature's rarest work : this lifeless all.
Oh ! fall some strange, unheard-of punishment
On Hesperus' head.

*Mor.*                    Hespérus, Hesperus; oh !
                    [*Falls back in his chair.*

*Hub.* Aye, 'twas his hand that wrought its pas-
        sage here,
And murdered love in its most sacred temple.
                    [LENORA *takes the body into her
                    lap and sits nursing it.*

*Hunts.* Alas! he heeds not; he is with his
        daughter.
Look at this other.

*Hub.*                    Oh ! I cannot bear it ;
Leave her ; a mother's agony is holy
As nature's mysteries.

*Hunts.*                    We'll to the Duke,
And crush the viper in his nest, before
Report alarm him.   Gently, gently tread
And wake not echo in this home of woe.
                *[Exeunt* HUBERT *and the* Huntsman.


*Len.*                [*Sings in a distracted manner.*
Lullaby, lullaby, sweet be thy sleep !
   Thou babe of my bosom, thou babe of my love :
Close, close to my heart, dear caresser, you creep,
   And kiss the fond eyelid that watches above.


One touch of those warm lips and then to bed.
Where is my child ?  I held her in my arms,
Her heart was beating in my bosom.   Ha ;
It is not she that lies upon my breast,
It is not she that whispers in my ear,
It is not she that kisses my salt cheek ;
They've stolen her from my couch and left this
          changeling,
Men call Despair—and she it is I suckle.
I know her by her killing lips of snow,
Her watery eyeballs and her tear-swoll'n cheeks.
My Floribel ! oh they have ta'en her soul
To make a second spring of it, to keep
The jarring spheres in melody.   Come, husband,
We'll wander up and down this wintry world,
And, if we see a sadder sight than this,
Or hear a tale, though false, of half such horror,
We'll closely hug our bosom-griefs in transport.
Why, husband !   You're asleep—you're deaf—
          you're dead !
I have not eyes enough to weep for both,

But I'll go steal the sleeping world's, and beg
A little dew from every sipping worm
To wet my cheeks with.             [*Exit.*


# ACT IV.

## SCENE I.

*An apartment in Orlando's palace.*

HESPERUS *alone.*

*Hesp.* How now? This quaint attire of coun-
  'tenance,
(Well fitted by prim Conscience's old tailor,
Hypocrisy,) sits rarely, and I'm here,
The affable, good bridegroom.   Wickedness,
How easy is thy lesson!   Now I stand
Up to the throat in blood; from Mercy's records
For evermore my guilty name is rased.
But yesterday, oh blessed yesterday,
I was a man;
And now—I start amazed at myself.
This hand, ay this it was I gave to Sin,
His grasp hath blasted it; 'twas made for kindness,
For gentle salutation, to deal out
Merciful alms, confirm the staff of age;
To reach the crust to want, the balm to sickness,
And balsam wounds; a limb of charity.
Now the wild adder's sting, the lightning's edge,
Are blunt and tame and gentle to it.   Psha!
Why then, men dread the adder and the flash;

So shall they cringe to me.   A step !   In haste
I've washed, and thought me spotless.   Yet I fear
Mine eye is so familiarized with blood,
It doth pass o'er and disregard the stains :
That recks not.   Sure I've brushed away those
   blushes,
And shaken hesitation from my tongue.

    *Enter* Attendant.

Menial, you're hasty in intruding thus.
Your errand ?
 *Attend.*  Lady Olivia—
 *Hesp.* Give me thine hand.   That name
Makes him my friend, who speaks it.   Say't again ;
Olivia, oh ! how each sweet syllable
Trickles along the tongue, an honied drop
Of harmony, Olivia.   I'll give all
The yellow wretchedness of human wealth
Unto the subtle artist, who shall teach
A clock to tell the seconds by that word ;
So shall I drive these frightful thoughts away,
And happiness—Do I look happy, sirrah ?
It matters not.   Speak on.
 *Attend.*    My lord, your bride—
 *Hesp.* Well sir, it was not I ; why lookest thou
  so ?
Beware.   Why layest thine hand across thy breast?
Is there a wound on't ?   Say.
 *Attend.*    A wound, my lord !
I understand not—
 *Hesp.*  Fool, I know thou dost not.
(If they would find it out, why let them dig
To hell's foundations.)   What !   Because I fold

Mine arms like any man unhurt, unhurting,
Must every slave suppose 'tis to conceal
Some fearful witness of a deed?
 *Attend.*     I thought not
'Twould anger thee; forgive me.
 *Hesp.*     Be it so;
It was too warmly said, for, as I trust,
You could not deem your master villain; never.
Yet say it were so, I but say suppose,
That I, whose clay is kneaded up with tears,
Had murdered, as you thought, some kindred
  creature;
Could not I wash the tokens of my guilt
From this outside, and show a hand as clean
As he who fingers first the air?
 *Attend.*     You might,
Till heaven's justice blasted you, be hid:
But leave these strange and ugly arguments;
The very fear would scare me from your side;
So banish them.
 *Hesp.*   Ay, they are strange indeed;
But mirth, believe me, mirth.   Come, tell me now,
How sits this ring?   Death! are your eyes nailed
  there?
Ha!   Does the ruby cast a sanguine shade
Across the veins?
 *Attend.*   Nought, save the splendid gem,
Amazed my sight; that's all.
 *Hesp.*    My friend, 'tis thine,
Too poor a recompense for the good tidings
Your tongue is laden with; now speak them out.
 *Attend.*  First let me bless you for your bounty,
  sir.

I came to call you to the wedding train,
Which waits without ; such smiles, on such rare
      faces,
Mine eyes have never seen : the bride is there ;
None but yourself is wanting to perfect
This sum of joy.
    *Hesp.*          Say I'll be there anon ;
And, mark me, on thy life forget each word
I just have spoken, blot them utterly
Out of thy mind ; I can reward a service.
I like thee well, my trusty, pleasant friend ;
Nay, pr'ythee go, there is no need of thanks.
                    [*Exit* Attendant.
I'll give that fellow's blab-tongue to the worms,
He's heard too much ; 'twere well to call him back,
And fasten down his memory with a dagger.
No, I'll not soil my skin again to-day ;
Down, Murder, down !
These untamed passions, that I keep about me,
Will thrive on naught save blood ; but they must
      fast,
And wear a specious tameness.  My Olivia,
How my whole soul is thine,—thine and the fiends'.
                        [*Exit.*


## SCENE II.

### *The interior of the Duke's palace.*

*Enter the* DUKE, HUBERT, *and the* Huntsman.

    *Duke.* Your tale hath stunned me with its dread-
    ful import,

And turned my every faculty to wonder.

*Hub.* You cannot doubt, my liege ?

*Duke.*                                    Hubert, I'd give
The best part of my power for hope to whisper
A no to my conviction.   Devilish villain !

*Hub.* Sure all good angels looked another way,
When this foul deed was done.

*Duke.*                                    All ancient cruelties
Look pale to it, and merciful : henceforth
They, that would christen human fiends, must write
Hesperus, 'stead of Cain ; and chiding nurses,
To still their peevish babes, shall offer them,
Not to the wolves, but him, the fiercer beast.

*Hub.* Oh ! my good lord, even now my sight is
          dimmed
With the salt gush, that came between my eyes
And that which seared them : on her turfy couch,
Like one just lulled into a heavy sleep,
Smiling and calm she lay ; the breath
Had not left fluttering up and down her bosom,
That, all blood-dabbled and besprent with gore,
Still held the guilty steel ; the name was on it
Of the accursed owner.

*Duke.*                                    Go, trusty Hubert,
Speed to Orlando's palace with my guard,
And drag the murderer here ; e'en now I'll judge
          him :
Be diligent, put wings upon your feet ;
Some vengeance will fall on us in the night,
If he remain unsentenced.                    [*Exeunt.*

## SCENE III.

### *A banqueting hall.*

LORD ERNEST, ORLANDO, CLAUDIO, OLIVIA, VIOLETTA, Lords, Ladies, *and* Attendants.

*L. Ern.* Sit here, my daughter; sit, and wel-
    come, all;
You shall not say my Hesperus' nuptial night
Lacks its due orgies.
    *Clau.*              Look upon the bride,
How blushes open their envermeiled leaves
On her fair features.
    *L. Ern.*         Sit, I pray you, sirs,
We will have deep and jovial carousal;
Put on the smiles of joy, and think of nought
But present pleasure, we've had woes enough;
Bid 'em be merry, daughter.
    *Oliv.*             Gentlemen,
My father wills me give you all a welcome,
And, if you love or honour our poor house,
Be glad with us.
    *Clau.* We thank your courtesy, lady, and obey.
    *L. Ern.* Where is this dilatory bridegroom
    still?
He was not wont to lag; what hast thou done
To banish him, Olivia?
    *Oliv.*           Good, my lord,
I fear his heart is ill. A veil of gloom
Darkens his cheeks, an anxious watchfulness

I.                                M

Plays in his eyes ; and, when he clasped my hand
Now in the chapel, though he smiled and whispered
Of bliss and love, an ague thrilled his veins,
And starting back he groaned.

   *L. Ern.*           Go, fetch him hither,
I warrant wine will cure him.

   *Attend.*          Here he comes.

### *Enter* HESPERUS.

   *Hesp.* (*aside*). What's all this blaze and riot ?
      Oh, a banquet.
They should have got me here the seven sins,
And all the evil things that haunt the world ;
Then what a goodly revel would we hold ;
E'en Death, while hastening to the sick man's
      pillow,
Should pause to listen our unhallowed talk,
And think us all the brood of Pestilence
Met in mysterious council.

   *Attend.*         Sir, your father
Has been enquiring for you, and desires
The comfort of your presence at the table.

   *Hesp.* The comfort of my presence !   Slave,
      thou mockest me.
Why dost thou thrust thy taper in my face ?
No price is set on't.

   *L. Ern.*        Hither, Hesperus ;
Thou dost not mark this company of kinsmen,
Met to congratulate you, and partake
Your gladness.

   *Hesp.*        Sirs, I thank you heartily.
(*Aside*) A curse upon the gaping saucy rabble ;
They must stare too.

*L. Ern.*　　　　Come, son, and sit beside me ;
They say you're ill, my boy.
　*Hesp.*　　　　　　　They say the truth.
*L. Ern.* What is your ailment ?
　*Hesp.*　　　　　　Life.　But here is one
Born to smile misery out of the world :
Look on me, my Olivia.
　*Oliv.*　　　　　　Dearest Hesperus,
Be calmer, I beseech you ; all are here
My friends, and yours.
　*Hesp.*　　No doubt.　They drain our goblets.
A friend ! What is't ? A thing shall squeeze your
　　　hand,
Caress with fervent love your broidered sleeve,
And wring his mouth into a leering lie,
While his heart damns thee.　One whose love's as
　　　deep
As your gold coffer.　Hast a wife ? They come ;
Buz, buz, lie, lie, the hungry meat-flies come,
" Dear lord, sweet lord, our only gentle lord ! "
Ay, thus they sugar o'er the silent dagger,
And love, and love, till they've inhelled thy soul.
Oh ! when I call for friend, bring honest poison.
Put out the lights, I like the beams o' th' moon ;
And tell those revellers to tope in silence.
　*L. Ern.* You would not overcast our best-meant
　　　mirth,
Bid us sit palled, like mourners at your bridal,
And hide in night our kindly countenances ?
　*Hesp.* Ay, by my grave I would.　There is on
　　　earth
One face alone, one heart, that Hesperus needs ;
'Twere better all the rest were not.　Olivia,

I'll tell thee how we'll 'scape these prying eyes ;
We'll build a wall between us and the world,
And in some summer wilderness of flowers,
As though but two hearts beat beneath the sun,
Consume our days of love.

   *L. Ern.*              I pray you, friends,
Excuse the wilful boy, his soul is wholly
Wrapt up in admiration of his bride :
We'll have her health ; come, fill your goblets
     round,
The bride, Olivia.

   *Clau.*          Happiness befall her,
May she ne'er feel a woe ; we drink to her.

                       [*Music.*

### *Enter* HUBERT.

   *Hub.* Hush, hush ;  ye ill-timed  sounds, let
     darkness come,
And with her funeral trappings hang the walls,
Or twilight lend a weak and fitful gleam,
That you may watch each others' watery cheeks.
Oh ! ladies, deck your beauties with salt diamonds,
Wail with the midnight wind, and look as sad
As if ye heard the thunder-voice of doom.

   *L. Ern.* What art thou, fearful man ?

   *Hub.*             Woe's harbinger ;
I come to bid you to a funeral ;
Prepare your eyes, for they must see dire ven-
     geance   .     -
Fall on the neck of crime.

   *Hesp.*          Turn out that fellow ;
I know him for a crazy marvel-monger,
A long-faced gossip, with his batch of wonders :

And now he'll tell you the most terrible news,
How many owls and ravens screeched last night,
Or how some ghost has left his marble tomb
To blab a drunken lie.
 *Hub.*     I tell a fiend
His guilt is hid no more. Ho ! there, the guard :

     *Enter* Guards.

That is your prisoner.
 *Hesp.*    You tread a scorpion :
The first that stirs brings to my sword his heart ;
Ye plunge into your graves.
       [*The* Guards *seize him.*
      Ah ! Floribel ;
Thou draggest my steel away, thou'st frozen me :
Girl, thou art pale.
 *L. Ern.*   How's this?
Ruffians, where do you bear my boy? Release him,
Or I'll——
 *Oliv.* Oh ! do not anger them. They're men
Who have sucked pity from their mothers' breasts,
They will not close their ears to my petition ;
And, if they'll loose him, I will pray for them
While speech is mine.
  *L. Ern.* Your swords, my friends, your swords.
  *Hub.* Stand back, my lords ; let the Duke's
    prisoner pass.
  *L. Ern.* The Duke ! what Duke dare seize my
    Hesperus?
My noble friends, my—sheath your coward swords,
And put your eyes upon the ground for fear,
Your Jove, the Duke he said ;—hear ye no
    thunder ?

But all the warriors of the universe
Shall not cow me : I'll free him ; villains, back.

*Hub.* Oh ! good old man ; alas ! he is a
murderer ?

*L. Ern.* A murderer ! (*drops his sword.*)  This
is a baby's arm.

*Oliv.* Save him, oh save him !  I am very faint.
　　　[ORLANDO, VIOLETTA, *and* Attendants
　　　　*carry her out.*

*Hesp.* Hence with that voice !  So shrieked—I
must not think.

*Hub.* Look to Lord Ernest.   The Duke sits in
council,
Waiting your presence, lords.   On, to the palace.
　　　[*Exeunt* CLAUDIO, HUBERT, HESPERUS,
　　　　Guards, Lords, *and* Ladies. *Manent*
　　　　LORD ERNEST *and* Attendants.

*L. Ern.* Where is he ?  What !  Ye traitors, let
him pass,
Chained, guarded ?  By this light—gird on your
swords.
My hairs are grey, but yet I've blood enough—
Did they not speak of crime ?  These limbs aren't
mine,
But some consumptive girl's.—Ay, it was murder !
I'll see the Duke—support me to the palace.
　　　　　　　　　　　　　　[*Exeunt.*

## SCENE IV.

*A street before the ducal palace.*

*Two* Guards *attending the body of* FLORIBEL ;
LENORA *hanging over it.*

1*st Guard.* 'Tis time to bear the body to the
    council :
The criminal is there already.
    2*nd Guard.*               Stay ;
'Twere sacrilege to shake yon mourner off,
And she will perish in the wintry night,
If unattended : yet this poor dumb witness
Is needful at the trial.   While she sleeps
With careful hands convey her to the Duke's,
And bid the women tend her.
    1*st Guard.*            Soft !   She breaks
Her trance, and rises like a new-born thing
Fresh from the realm of spirits.
    2*nd Guard.*          Hush ! she speaks.
    *Len.* I dreamed, and in that visioned agony
'Twas whispered by strange voices, like the dead's,
I was the mother of this Floribel,
And still a wanderer upon man's earth ;
No, no, I am her ghost, shade of her essence,
Thrust into some strange shape of womanhood
Until the tomb is open.   What are these ?
Good sir, have you a tear to throw away,
A little sigh to spare unto the wind ?
I've heard that there are hearts yet in the world,
Perhaps you have one.

*1st Guard.*                    Lady, for your sorrow
It aches most deeply.
  *Len.*                        Prithee, look you here.
Cold, cold; 'tis all in vain : those lustrous eyes
Will never beam again beneath the stars ;
Darkened for ever ; and those wan, dead lips :
They'll put her in the earth and let the world,
The pitiless bad world, tread o'er her beauty,
While I—ye airs of heaven, why will ye feed me ?
Why, ye officious ministers, bestow
The loathed blessing of a cursed existence ?
There's many a one now leans upon the cheek
Of his dead spouse, a-listening for her pulse,
And hears no motion but his bursting heart ;
Give him my life and bid him wipe his eyes.·
Look here, look here,
I've heard them call her flower ; oh ! had she been
The frailest rose that whitens in the blast,
Thus bruised and rifled by a ruffian hand,
I might have kept her living in my tears
A very little while, until I die ;
And then—now tell me this and I will bless thee,
Where thinkest our spirits go ?
  *1st Guard.*                    Madam, I know not ;
Some say they hang like music in the air,
Some that they sleep in flowers of Paradise,
Some that they lie ingirt by cloudy curtains,
Or 'mong the stars.
  *Len.*                   Oh ! not among the stars,
For, if she's there, my sight's so dimmed with tears,
I ne'er shall find her out,
But wander through the sparkling labyrinth
Wearied, alone ; oh ! say not 'mong the stars.

Why do ye move her?

*1st Guard.*            We must bear her hence
Unto the Duke.

*Len.*            What!   Is it not enough
That she is dead?

*1st Guard.*        No hand shall offer hurt,
And in short space we'll bring her back again,
Unto your cottage.

*Len.*        Thanks!   They shall not harm her;
Soldier, I will repay this kindness nobly;
Hark you; I'm going far off, to Paradise,
And if your child, or wife, or brother's there,
I'll bring them to you in your dreams some night.
Farewell; I will go search about for Comfort,
Him, that, enrobed in mouldering cerements, sits
At the grey tombstone's head beneath the yew;
Men call him Death, but Comfort is his name.

[*Exeunt.*

*Enter two* Citizens.

*1st Cit.* Well met sir, come you from the trial?

*2nd Cit.*                          Ay;
In wonder that the stones do not come down
To crush that monster of all wickedness,
The wretched Hesperus; there he stands,
Biting his chains and writhing in his rage
Like a mad tiger.

*1st Cit.*        Is he yet condemned?

*2nd Cit.* Death is the sentence.

*1st Cit.*                    See, the criminal
And his old father; what a sight of pity.

*Enter* HESPERUS *guarded,* ORLANDO, HUBERT,
LORD ERNEST, *and* Mob.

   *Hesp.* Well, gaping idiots; have ye stared
     enough;
Have ye yet satisfied your pious minds,
By thanking your most bounteous stars ye're not
A prodigy like this?   Get home and tell
Your wives, and put me in your tales and ballads;
Get home and live.
   *L. Ern.*        Oh hush my son,
Get some good priest of Charity to draw
Tears of repentance from your soul, and wake
The sleeping virtue.
   *Hesp.*       Who's this greybeard driveller?
Go, find your wits, old fellow, that bald skull
Is full of leaks; hence! look in last night's bowl;
Search all your money-bags: don't come abroad
Again without them; 'tis amiss.
   *L. Ern.*         Oh heavens!
Is this the son, over whose sleeping smiles
Often I bent, and, mingling with my prayers
Thanksgivings, blessed the loan of so much virtue.
   *Hesp.* That's right; weep on, weep on; for
     thou art he,
Who slew his only child, his first-born child.
   *Orl.* Oh look upon his galling agony,
These desperate yearnings of paternal love,
And try to have an heart.
   *Hesp.*       You're merry, friend;
Troth 'tis a goodly jest: what, dost thou think
These limbs, the strength of nature's armoury,
That but exist to dare, and dare the things

That make the blood of bravery turn pale
For very terror, such a minion's work,
The offspring of those dribbling veins?   Go to,
Thou'rt a sad idiot.

    *L Ern.* Oh! hear him not, thou ever-present
        Justice,
And close thy watchful eyelid, thou that weighest
Th' allotted scale of crime.

    *Hesp.*              Come hither, age;
I have a whisper for your secrecy;
Consider; who am I?

    *L. Ern.*         Thou wast my son,
The pulse of my dead heart, light of my eyes,
But now——

    *Hesp.*    Thy son! I would I'd time to laugh.
No, no; attend.   The night, that gave me being,
There was unearthly glee upon the winds,
There were strange gambols played beneath the
        moon,
The madman smiled uncouthly in his sleep,
And children shrunk aghast at goblin sights;
Then came a tap against the rattling casement,
Not the owl's wing, or struggle of the blast;
Thy dotardship snored loudly, and meanwhile
An incubus begot me.

    *L. Ern.*         Lead me home,
My eyes are dim; I cannot see the way:
I fain would sleep. [*Exit with some of the* Citizens.

    *Hesp.* Go, some one, tell his nurse
To get him swaddling clothes.

    *Orl.*         Prodigious wretch!
Rebel to man and heaven!   On thee shall fall
The cureless torture of the soul, the woe

Hell nurses for the deepest damned.

*Hesp.*                                          'Tis pity
So much good cursing should be thrown away;
Well spit, my reptile!   Officers, lead on:
Shall I, in bondage, stand to glut the sight
Of these poor marvel-dealing things?   Away,
I'll shut them out; the red death on you all!

                                        [*Going.*

Ah! my good fellow, are you of the train
That wait upon Olivia?

*Attend.*  I'm her servant.

*Hesp.*  How fares she?

*Attend.*                          Very ill; she wastes,
Careless of living.

*Hesp.*              Tell her, on my love
I charge her live; oh heaven, *she* must not die,
There are enough accusers in the tomb.
Tell her——Shame, shame, they shall not see me
          weep.                              [*Exeunt.*

## ACT V.

### Scene I.

*A room in Mordred's cottage.*

*The dead* FLORIBEL *laid upon a couch.*
LENORA *and* Boy.

*Len.* Why dost thou weep, thou little churl?
*Boy.*                         Alas !
I need not say.
   *Len.* Boy, boy; thou'rt wicked ; thou wouldst
      have me think
I have no Floribel, but thou shalt see
How I will make her live.
                  It is the morning,
And she has risen to tend her favourite flowers,
And, wearied with the toil, leans o'er her seat
In silent languor.   Now I will steal in,
Softly : perchance she sleeps.   It's plain she hears
      not,
Or she would leap all-smiling to my arms ;
I wish dear Mordred were awake to see
How the sweet girl will start and welcome me,
At my first speaking : but I'll wait awhile,
And save the pleasure.   Ah ! thou pretty silence,
I know thou'rt thinking what a happy cot
'Twill be when our loved patient is quite well.

Yes, you shall take him his first walk ; he'll lean
Upon that arm, and you shall show the plants
New set in the garden, and the grassy path
Down to the church.

              Now I will stand behind her,
So,—she must drop her head upon my bosom,
As she looks up.   Good-morrow to thee, sweet ;
Now for her gentle cry ; she's turning round.
No—for she wont seem startled, but pretend
To have heard my coming.   Why art thou so slow ?
Sweet little wag, I know thou'rt not asleep.
Soft !   'Tis the swiftness of my thought outruns
Her proper motions.   I've this instant spoken,
The air has scarcely yet ta'en up my words ;
May be she hears not.   But I did not speak ;
'Twas only thought, or whispered.   Child, good-
     morrow ;
Yes, she hears that, but will not stir even yet.
I'll not be frightened, for she surely hears ;
Though, if I had not seen her garments move,
And caught the tiny echo of her breath,
'Twere dreadful.   Speak, I pray thee, Floribel,
Speak to thy mother ; do but whisper " ay ; "
Well, well, I will not press her ; I am sure
She has the welcome news of some good fortune,
And hoards the telling till her father comes ;
Perhaps she's found the fruit he coveted
Last night.   Ah ! she half laughed.   I've guessed
     it then ;
Come tell me, I'll be secret.   Nay, if you mock me,
I must be very angry till you speak.
Now this is silly ; some of those young boys
Have dressed the cushions with her clothes in sport.

'Tis very like her.   I could make this image
Act all her greetings ; she shall bow her head,
" Good-morrow mother ; " and her smiling face
Falls on my neck.—Oh, heaven, 'tis she indeed !
I know it all—don't tell me.


## Scene II.

*The interior of a prison.*

HESPERUS *alone.*

*Hesp.* Hark ! Time's old iron voice already
        counts
The steps unto the after-world, o'er which
Sleep in her arms hath carried man to-night ;
And all it wakes to business or to joy,
Save one ; and, mingled with its solemn tone,
I heard the grating gates of hell expand——
Oh ! house of agony,
I feel thy scorching flames already near.
Where shall I 'scape ?   Is there no hiding place ?
Spirit, that guidest the sun, look round this ball,
And through the windows of deep ocean's vault ;
Is there no nook just big enough for me ?
Or, when I'm dead, can I not pass my soul
For common air, and shroud me in some cloud ?
But then the earth will moulder, clouds evanish ;
So Hell, I must unto thee, darksome vale ;
For dared I hope, I could not wish, Elysium :
There should I meet the frowns of Floribel ;
My father would be there : black gulph of anguish,
Thou art far better than such paradise.

Why did they teach me there is such a place?
The pang of misery is there; I know
There is a land of bliss, and am not in it;
This, this outstings your lashes, torturers;
He has no lack of punishment who feels it.

.       *Enter* Jailor.

Oh! speak not for a moment, speak not, sir,
I know thine errand well; so tell it not.
But let me shut mine eyes, and think a little
That I am what I was.   Ay, there he sits,
My good old sire, with his large eye of love.
How well it smiles upon that lovely maid,
A beauteous one, indeed; and yet, they say,
She died most cruelly.   Oh! tell me something,
Drive out these dreams.
   *Jail.*        Prisoner, prepare for death. [*Exit.*
   *Hesp.* Death! Death! What's death? I can-
    not think.

*Enter* LENORA.

Who art thou?
   *Len.* Ha! knowest thou not the wretch thou'st
    made Lenora?
Alone I've found thee, villain.
   *Hesp.*                    Not alone;
Oh! not alone: the world hath burst its ribs,
And let out all the demons in the pit;
Thick; thick they throng: I cannot breathe for
    them;
The hounds of Lucifer are feeding on me,
Yet I endure; Remorse and Conscience too,
Stirring the dying embers of my heart,

Which Passion hath burnt out, like midnight
    gossips
Sit idly chattering of the injured dead ;
But thou'rt the last and worst ; I hoped to hide
Beneath the turf from thee.
    *Len.* Thou shalt not leave me ; stand and hear‘
        my curse,—
Oh such a curse·! I learned it from a voice
That wandered 'mid the damned : it burns my
    tongue,
Listen, wretch, listen ;
Thus, thus I curse thee . . . . No, I do revoke it,
My pardon be upon you for your deeds ;
Though thou didst stab me through my Floribel,
I think thou once didst love her ; didst thou not ?
    *Hesp.* With my whole soul, as now I worship
        her.
    *Len.* Alas ! say no; I wish thou'dst break my
        heart ;
Now pr'ythee do ; I'll bless thee for't again.
    *Hesp.* What ! is it stubborn yet ? Then thou
        canst teach me
How to bear misery——but I need it not,
They've dug my grave.
    *Len.*               But, while you still are living,
What say you to some frolic merriment ?
There are two grassy mounds beside the church,
My husband and my daughter ; let us go
And sit beside them, and learn silence there ;
Even with such guests we'll hold our revelry
O'er bitter recollections : there's no anguish,
No fear, no sorrow, no calamity,
In the deathful catalogue of human pains,   ·
   I.                                     N

But we will jest upon't, and laugh and sing :
Let pitiful wretches whine for consolation,
Thank heaven we despair.

*Enter* Guards.

*Hesp.*                       See you these men ?
They bid me to a strange solemnity.
  *Len.* Must thou be gone ?
  *Hesp.*                    I must, alas ! for ever.
Live and be blessed, mother of Floribel.
                        [*Exit with* Guards.
  *Len.* Farewell ; farewell.  They drag him to the
        scaffold,
My son, the husband of my Floribel :
They shall not slaughter him upon the block,
And to the cursing multitude hold up
The blackened features which she loved ; they
        shall not.                    [*Exit.*


SCENE III.

*An apartment in Orlando's palace.*

OLIVIA, VIOLETTA, *and* Attendants.

  *Oliv.* Sing me that strain, my gentle Violet,
Which erst we used, in sport and mockery
Of grief, beneath the willow shade at eve
To chaunt together ; 'twill allay my woes.


SONG, *by two voices.*

*First Voice.*
Who is the baby, that doth lie

Beneath the silken canopy
Of thy blue eye?

*Second.*

It is young Sorrow, laid asleep
In the crystal deep.

*Both.*

Let us sing his lullaby,
Heigho ! a sob and a sigh.

*First Voice.*

What sound is that, so soft, so clear,
Harmonious as a bubbled tear
Bursting, we hear?

*Second.*

It is young Sorrow, slumber breaking,
Suddenly awaking.

*Both.*

Let us sing his lullaby,
Heigho ! a sob and a sigh.

*Oliv.* 'Tis well : you must not weep ; 'twill
    spoil your voices,
And I shall need them soon.
*Viol.*                       For what, Olivia ?
You were not wont to prize our simple skill
Erewhile so highly : what will please you most?
What lay of chivalry, or rural sport,
Or shepherd love, shall we prepare you next?
*Oliv.* My dirge : I shall not tax your music else.
It must be : wherefore weep?

*Viol.*                              I cannot help it,
When you converse so mournfully of death;
You must forgive me.
   *Oliv.*                    Death! thou silly girl,
There's no such thing; 'tis but a goblin word,
Which bad men conjure from their reeking sins
To haunt their slumbers; 'tis a life indeed.
These bodies are the vile and drossy seeds,
Whence, placed again within their kindred earth,
Springs Immortality, the glorious plant
Branching above the skies.   What is there here
To shrink from?   Though your idle legends tell
How cruelly he treats the prostrate world;
Yet, unto me, this shadowy potentate
Comes soft and soothing as an infant's sleep,
And kisses out my being.   Violetta,
Dost thou regard my wish, perhaps the last?
   *Viol.* Oh! madam, can you doubt it? We have
       lived
Together ever since our little feet
Were guided on the path, and thence have shared
Habits and thoughts.   Have I in all that time,
That long companionship, e'er thwarted thee?
Why dost thou ask me then?   Indeed I know not
Thy wishes from my own, but to prefer them.
Then tell me what you will; if its performance
But occupy the portion of a minute,
'Twill be a happy one, for which I thank you.
   *Oliv.* Thine hand upon it; I believe thy pro-
      mise.
When I am gone you must not weep for me,
But bring your books, your paintings, and your
      flowers,

And sit upon my grassy monument
In the dewy twilight, when they say souls come
Walking the palpable gross world of man,
And I will waft the sweetest odours o'er you ;
I'll shower down acorn-cups of spicy rain
Upon your couch, and twine the boughs above ;
Then, if you sing, I'll take up Echo's part,
And from a far-off bower give back the ends
Of some remembered airy melody ;
Then, if you draw, I'll breathe upon the banks
And freshen up the flowers, and send the birds,
Stammering their madrigals, across your path ;
Then, if you read, I'll tune the rivulets,
I'll teach the neighbouring shrubs to fan your
    temples,
And drive sad thoughts and fevers from your
    breast ;
But, if you sleep, I'll watch your truant sense,
And meet it in the fairy land of dreams
With my lap full of blessings; 'twill, me-
    thinks,
Be passing pleasant, so don't weep for me.
    *Viol.* I fear, Olivia, I'm a selfish creature,
These tears drop not for you, but for myself;
'Tis not that death will have you, but that I
Shall be a lone lost thing without your love.
    *Oliv.* My love will spread its wings for ever near
    you ;
Each gentler, nobler, and diviner thought
Will be my prompting.
    *Viol.*        Well, I'll bear it then,
And even persuade myself this intercourse
Of disembodied minds is no conjecture,

No fiction of romance.   The summer sun
Will find me on the sod that covers you,
Among the blossoms ; I'll try not to cry ;
And when I hear a rustle in the grass,
Or the soft leaves come kissing my bent arm,
I shall not lay it to the empty air,
But think I know thy utterance in the noises
That answer me, and see thy rosy fingers
Dimpling the brooks.

    *Oliv.*               Thou wilt be cheerful, then ?

    *Viol.* Yes, with this hope,
That when, some silent, melancholy night,
I've sobbed myself to sleep over your picture,
Or some memorial of your former kindness,
I shall awaken to ethereal music,
And find myself a spirit with Olivia. [*A bell tolls.*

    *Oliv.* Whose summons loads the gale with
        mournful sound ?

    *Attend.* Dear lady ?

    *Oliv.*         I ask who's dead or who's to die :
You need not tell me : I remember now,—
It was a thought I wished to keep away.
My love, my Hesperus, unto me thou wert
The gentlest and the kindest ; sudden madness
Must have inspired this deed ; and why do I,
Wife of the dying, tarry in the world ?
I feel already dissolution's work ;
A languor creeps through all my torpid veins ;
Support me, maidens.

    *Viol.*             Come unto your couch ;
Sleep will recruit thee.

    *Oliv.*             Yes, the breathless sleep ;
Come and pray round me, as I fade away ;

My life already oozes from my lips,
And with that bell's last sound I shall expire.

[*Exeunt.*

## SCENE IV.

### *The place of Execution.*

HESPERUS, *guarded*, HUBERT, ORLANDO,
Citizens, *&c.*

*Hesp.* Now in the scornful silence of your features
I see my hated self; my friends, I was
The pestilence you think of; but to-night
Angelic ministers have been with me,
And by the holy communings of conscience
Wrought a most blessed change; my soul has wept
And lain among the thorns of penitence;
I ask, (and you will not refuse the boon
To one who cannot crave again) forgiveness
For all that in the noontide of my crimes,
Against you, even in thought, I have committed.

*Orl.* And we rejoice to grant it; and if prayers,
In meek sincerity outpoured, avail,
You have them from our hearts.

*Hesp.* Thy sister's soul spake in those words,
Orlando;
A wretch's blessing for them.  I'm as one
In some lone watch-tower on the deep, awakened
From soothing visions of the home he loves;
Trembling he hears the wrathful billows whoop,
And feels the little chamber of his life

Torn from its vale of clouds, and, as it falls,
In his midway to fate, beholds the gleam
Of blazing ships, some swallowed by the waves,
Some, pregnant with mock thunder, tossed abroad,
With mangled carcases, among the winds ;
And the black sepulchre of ocean, choaked
With multitudinous dead ; then shrinks from pangs,
Unknown but destined.    All I know of death
Is, that 'twill come.    I have seen many die
Upon the battle field, and watched their lips
At the final breath, pausing in doubt to hear
If they were gone.    I have marked oftentimes
Their pale eyes fading in the last blue twilight ;
But none could speak the burning agony,
None told his feelings.    I ne'er dreamed I died,
Else might I guess the torture that attends it.
But men unhurt have lost their several senses,
Grown deaf, and blind, and dumb without a pang
And surely these are members of the soul,
And, when they fail, man tastes a partial death :
Besides our minds share not corporeal sleep,
But go among the past and future, or perhaps
Inspire another in some waking world,
And there's another death.
I will not fear ; why do ye linger, guards ?
I've flung my doubts away ; my blood grows wild.

   *Hub.* The hour appointed is not yet arrived,
Some moments we must wait ; I pray you, patience.

   *Enter* LORD ERNEST *in the dress of a peasant,*
        *followed by* CLAUDIO.

   *Clau.* My lord, where dost thou hurry ?
   *L. Ern.*                To Despair ;

Away ! I know thee not.   Henceforth I'll live
Those bitter days that Providence decrees me,
In toil and poverty.   Oh son, loved son,
I come to give thee my last tear and blessing ;
Thou wilt not curse the old, sad wretch again ?

 *Hesp.* (*Falling upon the ground and covering*
    *himself with the loose earth.*)

   Oh trample me to dust.

 *L. Ern.* (*Lying down beside him.*)

        My own dear child ;
Ay, we will lie thus sweetly in the grave,
(The wind will not awake us, nor the rain,)
Thou and thy mother and myself ; but I,
Alas ! I have some tearful years to come,
Without a son to weep along with me.

 *Hesp.* Father, dear father !
And wilt thou pray for me ?  Oh, no ! thou canst
  not,
Thou must forget or hate me.

 *L. Ern.*       Sirs, have pity ;
Let him not use me thus.   Hesperus, Hesperus,
Thou'rt going to thy mother ; tell her, son,
My heart will soon be broken ; so prepare
To have me with you.   Bless thee, boy, good night.
            [*Exit.*

 *Hesp.* My father, heaven will curse thee if I bless ;
But I shall die the better for this meeting. [*Kneeling.*
Oh, Floribel ! fair martyr of my fury,
Oh, thou blessed saint ! look down and see thy
  vengeance,
And, if thy injured nature still can pity,
Whisper some comfort to my soul.   'Tis done ;
I feel an airy kiss upon my cheek ;

It is her breath; she hears me; she descends;
Her spirit is around me.   Now I'll die.

*Enter* LENORA.

*Len.* Where's Hesperus?  Not gone?  Speak to
    me loud,
I hear not for the beating of my heart.
We're not both dead?  Say thou hast 'scaped the
    headsman,
Nor felt the severing steel fall through thy neck.

*Hesp.* I stay one moment for the signal here,
The next I am no more.

*Len.*               Then we have conquered.
Friend, leave us : I would speak a private word
Unto thy prisoner.   Look upon these flowers;
They grew upon the grave of Floribel,
And, when I pulled them, through their tendrils
    blew
A sweet soft music, like an angel's voice.
Ah ! there's her eye's dear blue ; the blushing down
Of her ripe cheek in yonder rose ; and there
In that pale bud, the blossom of her brow,
Her pitiful round tear ; here are all colours
That bloomed the fairest in her heavenly face ;
Is't not her breath ?

*Hesp.* (*smelling them.*)   It falls upon my soul
Like an unearthly sense.

*Len.*              And so it should,
For it is Death thou'st quaffed :
[1] I steeped the plants in a magician's potion,
More deadly than the scum of Pluto's pool,
Or the infernal brewage that goes round

---

[1] The reader will recollect Massinger's "Duke of Milan."

From lip to lip at wizards' mysteries ;
One drop of it, poured in a city conduit,
Would ravage wider than a year of plague ;
It brings death swifter than the lightning shaft.

   *Hesp.* 'Tis true : I feel it gnawing at my heart,
And my veins boil as though with molten lead.
How shall I thank thee for this last, best gift ?

   *Len.* What is it rushes burning through my
      mouth ?
Oh ! my heart's melted.—Let me sit awhile.

   *Hub.* Hear ye the chime ? ,Prisoner, we must
      be gone ;
Already should the sentence be performed.

   *Hesp.* On ! I am past your power.
             (*To Lenora.*) How farest thou now ?

   *Len.* Oh ! come with me, and view
These banks of stars, these rainbow-girt pavilions,
These rivulets of music—hark, hark, hark !
And here are winged maidens floating round,
With smiles and welcomes ; this bright beaming
      seraph
I should remember ; is it not——my daughter ?
                      [*Dies.*

   *Hesp.* I see not those ; but the whole earth's in
      motion ;
I cannot stem the billows ; now they roll :
And what's this deluge ? Ah ! Infernal flames !
                      [*Falls.*

   *Hub.* Guards, lift him up.

   *Hesp.* The bloody hunters and their dogs !
      Avaunt—
Tread down these serpents' heads. Come hither,
      Murder ;

Why dost thou growl at me? Ungrateful hound!
Not know thy master? Tear him off! Help!
    Mercy!
Down with your fiery fangs!—I'm not dead yet.
                       [*Dies.*

# THE IMPROVISATORE.

["The Improvisatore, in three fyttes, with other Poems.
By Thomas Lovell Beddoes. Oxford: printed for J. Vincent,
near Brasennose College; and G. and W. B. Whittaker, Ave
Maria Lane, London. 1821. 128 pp." This volume is now
for the first time reprinted. Beddoes endeavoured, and with
an approach to success, to suppress all traces of its having
existed. "It was his wont to leave, intact in its externals
(some gay binding perhaps of his own selection), but
thoroughly eviscerated, every copy on which he could lay
his hands."]

## THE INDUCTION
## TO THE FIRST FYTTE.

DANK is the air and dusk the sky,
The snow is falling featherily,
And, as the light flakes kiss the ground,
They dance in mazy circles round ;  ·
Like venturous nestlings in the shower,
Trying their new-fledged pinions' power.
The boughs ice-sheathed shake, bristling out,
And coral holly berries pout
In crystal cradles, like the shine
Of goblets flushed with blood-red wine :
Whilst whistling breezes hurry by,
Snow-clad December's feeble cry,
And the pale moonlight downward twirls,
Riding upon the snow's cold curls.
The subtle net of mist is wove,
And all below, and all above
Are twinkling through it, the stars beam
With many a flash and fitful gleam,
Like gold-scaled fishes struggling
In flimsy purse of fisher's ring.
Within the hall is banquet high,

Dazzling with torch and ladies' eye ;
Rich wine, with steaming wavelets' swell,
Is bubbling in its silver well,
And from the hearths warm streamlets flow
Of cheerful heat and flickering glow ;
With murmur loud the rebel fire
Is spitting forth its flameful ire,
Licking with curled fang the bar,
And reeking in the strife of war,
And waving through the smoke-dimmed air
Its blazing banner of red glare :
With spicy wreaths the goblet's crowned,
And jests and laughter sparkle round.
Such feasts of joy and ease repay
The toil and dulness of the day,
And lighten the dull hours of even,
Like stars that gild the dome of heaven.
" Now for a tale," exclaimed the Knight,
" Breathing the love of ladies bright,
And virtues high and sorrow deep,
Till music's self shall seem to weep :       .
Call forth that wandering minstrel boy,
That with his lyre-string loves to toy."
The youth was brought, and low he bowed
Modestly to the noble crowd.
" Strike," quoth the Knight, " some simple tune,
Like blackbird's song in leafy June ;
And veil the words you chaunt aloud
Of love, or war, in music's cloud,"
He said.   With finger springing light
To joyous sounds, the songster wight
First tuned his lyre, then danced along       .
Amid the mazy paths of song.

# ALBERT AND EMILY.

### I.

'TWAS on the evening of a summer day,
The frowning clouds were scudding fast away;
The sky, which shone like one broad eye of blue,
Sprinkled the velvet turf with scented dew:
    The prattling birds now ventured from their
        nests,—
      Some spread their wings where the sweet balm
        was shed,
    Some vainly decked their variegated breasts,
      And some were bustling to their tiny bed.

### II.

There was a flush of gladness in the west,
The sun was sinking from the realms he blessed;
Huge snaky wreaths of mist were twining round
In spires, the steaming incense of the ground:
    The flowrets downward cast their tearful eyes,
      And seemed to sleep, so silently they hung;
    Save where the harebells waved in zephyr's
        sighs;
      To elfin ears, no doubt, a peal they rung.

### III.

The valley was all motionless and still;
A sleepy streamlet murmured down the hill,
And on its mossy banks the violet blue,
The couch of perfume, in dark beauty grew.

I.                                            O

In the mid stream there was a little isle,
  Fragrant and cool, with liquid odours wet ;
Round it the dimpled current seemed to smile ;
  'Twas like a gem in living silver set.


### IV.

Within that isle there was a flower-crowned mount
For ever moistened by a sparkling fount ;
'Twas as though Flora had been sporting there,
And dropped some jewels from her loosened hair :
  On many a spangled stalk there blushed the rose,
    And in its cup a drop of evening dew
  Looked like a cloud-wept ruby, among those
    The silken grass its tears of emerald threw.


### V.

There too were lilies, like a lady's cheek
Moistened with lover's kisses ; there the sleek
And glittering turf was daisy-chequered o'er,
A beauteous carpet on the arbour's floor.
  And there they lay, Albert and Emily,
    As fair a pair of buds as e'er were seen,      .
  The while she listened to his eager sigh,
    · And answered, smiling, all his glances keen.


### VI.

Her eyes were but half open, yet out peeped
Two starry balls, in watery radiance steeped,
Between the fringèd lids, striving to hide
Their softness from the lover at her side :
  And when he dared to look into those bright
    And streaming crystals, with a timid stare,
  He saw a smiling babe swathed in their light,
    As if the god of love were cradled there.

### VII.

Those eyes were of a beauteous, melting blue,
Like a dark violet bathed in quivering dew ;
Her mouth seemed formed for sighs and sportive
            guile
And youthful kisses ; and there played a smile
    About her lips ; like an inconstant moth
        Around a flower, now settling, and now flown
    With every passing breath, as though 'twere
            loth
        To stay and make the resting-place its own.

### VIII.

Her bosom too was fair, and calmly heaved
As her glad ears his fervent vows received ;
And ever and anon a flush was cast
Across its surface, as his warm sighs passed.
    But, underneath that breast, panted a heart
        In which pure love had fixed his sovereign
            seat ;
    All ignorant of cold disdain or smart,
        Responsive to her lover's sighs it beat.

### IX.

Her music-winged voice, from her sweet throat,
Came winding to the ear, like a small boat
Of sounds melodious buoyed upon a lake
Of flowing harmony ; and, when she spake,
    Echo scarce sighed again, or breathed a sound
        As soft as zephyrs buzzing in a tree ;
    Or, as in noontide stillness float around
        The honey-smothered murmurs of a bee.

### X.

Adown her fair and glowing cheek there hung
A cluster of slight auburn curls, that clung
To her brows tenderly ; a brilliancy
Fell on them from the sunshine of her eye ;
   And, as she calmly breathed, those ringlets gay
    Danced in her sighs upon her bosom white ;
   So oft the wanderer in the noon of May
    Sees golden insects glittering in the light.

### XI.

He was a fair and noble youth ; his face
Was feminine, and yet a manly grace
Adorned his features, and imperial thought
Sate on his lofty brow, whereon were wrought
   The lineaments of wisdom ; but a cloud
    Of love despondent oftentimes would lie
   Across his front, and kindle up a proud
    Swift flash of lightning in his lowering eye.

### XII.

Vows panted on his breath, and the soft air
Grew moist with dewy sighs which floated there ;
Their eyes were quaffing one another's beams,
Fixedly feasting on those amorous streams.
   'Twas on the evening of a summer day,
    A joyous moment in a youthful life,
   When Albert to his heart, as there she lay,
    Clasped that bright Angel upon earth, a wife.

### XIII.

(For they were plighted ; and the sunset ray
That kissed her lovely bosom, the next day

Would light them to the changing of their troth,
So long desired and waited for by both.)
    He read in those deep glances, which the lash
        So beautifully curtained from his sight,  .
    Her perfect love, and answered with a flash
        Of rapture from his eye, which streamed
            delight.


### XIV.

Meantime the sun was fading fast away,
Stealing his glory from the closing day ;
The breeze low murmured with its downy breath,
And fanned the songsters into nightly death.
    The glare of light was mellowed into shade,
        And myriad-eyed night, the queen of thought,
    The silent mandate of old time obeyed,
        And blotted nature's beauties into nought.


### XV.

Quickly the moon, in virgin lustre dight,
Amongst the brilliant swarm cast forth her light,
Sailing along the waveless lake of blue,
Smiling with pallid light, a bright canoe.
    The earth beneath,—the silent-moving globe,—
        The restless sea, the hills, and fertile ground,
    Were all enveloped in a slender robe
        Of splendour, which she nightly weaves
            around.


### XVI.

Still there the lovers were, and her hand lay,
Wrapped round and round, by his, in gentle play :

It struggled softly, with a feeble power,
Like a lone bee imprisoned in a flower,
   That beats against the petals peevishly ;
     Yet round her wrist still Albert's fingers clung,
  And, as she looked at him half angrily,
     To soothe her, with a murmuring voice he
      sung.

### XVII.

But oh ! what thought-dipped pen shall chain in
     words
Those sweet endearments, that, like truant birds,
Fled from their lips, and nestled in their ears,
Unruffled by sad sobs, unclogged with tears ?
   What voice shall echo lovers' gentle jars,
     And fancied griefs, and eager sighs, which stole
  Airy-winged prisoners through mouth's ivory
     bars,
     And whispers, bubbles of the melting soul ?

### XVIII.

Those words that waft the odour of the heart,
Those looks which chain their eyes together?—Art
Is all in vain.   My young and feeble hand
Drops from its nerveless grasp the poet's wand.
   Then let your feelings tell them all in thought ;
     And to th' Æolian touches of the lyre
  Hang the sweet tear, from Love's deep treasury
     brought,
     And tune the breathings of his cherub choir.

### XIX.

She listened to his love, and wove a wreath
For her young bard, of plants which grew beneath ;

She kissed them as she plucked, and tried to shower
Upon his willing head each lovely flower.
   Her head was pillowed on her waxen arm,
     And to the light she turned her forehead bare,
    And slumber'd lightly.   Oh, what impious harm
     Could dare to harass that sweet sleeping fair !

### xx.

The murmuring brook, and breezes without number,
Lulled with short harmony her peaceful slumber :
Then Albert looked with joy upon his love,
And called on her sweet visions from above :
   And, ere he turned to sleep, he swept aside
     The long grass from her cheeks, and gently
      spread
   His mantle, which was warm and fully wide,
    Upon her bosom and unshielded head.

### XXI.

They slept like infants.   Not a breeze passed o'er
Their cheeks, but downy lullings with it bore :
Their calm lips moved not, and no throb of pain
Drove fitful streams from every swelling vein
   To tinge with blood the fever-parched cheek,
     But the thin moonlight kissed their eyes to rest,
    And, like a mother's blessing, pure and meek,
     It hovered o'er them in their silent nest.

### XXII.

But in their dreams, which thickly came and sweet,
They knew not with what sudden sweep a fleet
Of clustering clouds, cumbering the stars, were
       driven,
And scowled upon their slumbers from high heaven :

, They poured unnumberèd, until the sky
Was blotted every where: there seemed to stare
At intervals an hideous bloodshot eye,
That threatened them with flickering, doubtful
flare.

### XXIII.

At length the war-cry of the heavens burst out,
A deep, encreasing murmur; like the shout
From darkling ambush of some savage foes:
At that loud peal the startled hills arose,
And growled out discord from their straining
throats:
The clouds again gave forth a dismal roar;
Again the mountains caught the deafening notes,
Like surges lashing on a rocky shore.

### XXIV.

And when those billows of fierce sound had passed,
Chasing their echo on the midnight blast,
A sullen silence brooded on the hill,
And every living thing was deadly still:
The air grew stagnant, not a truant breath
Ruffled the herbage; every sound was hushed
On earth and sky, as if the hand of death
Had, with wild grasp, all life and motion
crushed.

### XXV.

Then Emily awoke. She, in her sleep,
Had seen bright angel faces downward peep
With radiant kindness, and she seemed to hear
Whispers of comfort rustle in her ear;

Her soul was bathed in gladness ; every thought,
   That formed a picture in her clouded eye,
Fresh joy and pleasure to her feelings brought :
   She woke—and saw the terrors of the sky !

### XXVI.

Fear choaked her screams ; she flew and rudely
     took
Reclining Albert by his arm, and shook
The sleeper with her weak and trembling might,
That he might know the dangers of the night.
   She stirred him ; but he 'woke not—Oh ! that
     sleep,
     'Twould never leave him ; slowly she laid
     down
   His heavy arm, and then began to weep ;
     He started up, and saw the tempest frown.—

### XXVII.

As he was rising quickly from the ground,
She heard him move, and gladly turned around;
He clasped her hand ;—'twas trembling and chill,
But between his he wrapped it fondly still.
   She tried to whisper to him all her dread,
     The stifled words fell back into her breast;
   Then on his arm she softly drooped her head,
     Which to his swelling heart he silent pressed.

### XXVIII.

He murmured comfort in her ear, and chid
The sorrow which her shivering bosom hid,
Then gently bore her with uplifted arm
From clouds which glared with thunder and with
     harm.

Near them an oak in sturdy strength uprose,
　And proudly stretched a bulky trunk of power;
Quick to that spot the harassed lover goes,
　　To shield his precious burthen from the
　　　shower.


### XXIX.

The clouds anew with fury 'gan to swell,
Till from their depths sprung forth an hideous yell,
Darting along the wind, stunning the earth,
And echoing horribly with fiendish mirth.
　The parting clouds that hovered in the heaven'
　　Wild cataracts of tempest downward threw,
　The veil of darkness in the midst was riven,
　　And the swift blast with wings of lightning
　　　flew.


### XXX.

Pale Emily said nothing, but she wept,
And shuddering into his bosom crept;
There in despair she closed her deafened ear,
And sought a false security from fear.
　He thought upon the lovely one that laid
　　Her helpless beauty on his trusty heart,
　And muttered hope to the distracted maid,
　　Resolving that in death they ne'er should
　　　part.


### XXXI.

She heard not what he said, but yet she smiled
Because she heard his tones; with terror wild,
Close to his beating bosom still she clung,
And nestled in his vest her head, that hung.

He tried again to speak, again to cheer
  The timid girl ; but his grief-blighted voice
Withered upon his tongue ; and freezing fear
  Crept to her heart 'midst the appalling noise.


### XXXII.

They stood entwined together.   With a shock
The thunder ceased, and, like a parted rock,
The darkness split asunder : a huge mouth
Seemed to be yawning wide, with grin uncouth ;—
  It was a deep and roaring grave of fire !
    She heard a sudden crash, she felt him start,
   And thought he gasped a groan; she drew him
        nigher,
    And fierce with horror pressed against his heart.


### XXXIII.

It throbbed but slowly; now it seemed to stay
It's faultering beat—quickly she turned away,
And hushed her breathing, but she heard no sound,
She felt no fluttering of his breath around.
  His arms froze stiff about her—when she spoke
   He answered not again; she tried to shriek,
   And started back; he fell against the oak,
    And never soothed her, or essayed to speak.


### XXXIV.

She bent her ear close to him on the ground,
And strained with pain to listen—there's no sound.
She whispered, he replied not ; wildly bold,
She clasped his hand, but it was clammy cold ;

Nerveless it dropped upon his upward side.
  She pressed with both her arms his silent
    head ;
Some fiendish tongue close in her hearing cried,
  With death-like accent, " Mourn for Albert
    dead ! "

### XXXV.

With terror-stricken eyes she looks behind,—
Is't fiendish laughter that bestrides the wind ?
And, hark again ! a wild and fearful knell,
Another dismal, superhuman yell !
  She turns ; a sea of faces meet her view,—
    Foaming, distorted features far and near,
  Lolling their tongues, that reek with sulphur
    blue,—
    Into her melting eyes with gibes they peer.

### XXXVI.

She feels her forehead glow, her bosom burn.
Unhappy lovely one ! and where to turn
She knows not ; for her eyes, before so bright,
Are dimmed and dazzled at the wizard sight.
  She felt her quivering heart with pain grow
    sick,
    It withered in her breast and died away ;
 Her throat was cloggèd and her breath came
    thick ;
    She tottered down and by her lover lay.

### XXXVII.

Next morn the bridemaids found the hapless pair ;
She met them first, and with an idiot stare

Gazed on them, and rushed on ; then gambolled
 back,
To lead them swiftly through the well-known
 track.
 They passed along the valley, o'er the hill,
  After her beck—but not a word she spoke.
 She brought them to the island, there stood
  still,
  And pointed wildly to the scattered oak.


### XXXVIII.

Looking that way, she burst into a roar
Of hideous laughter, then they hurried o'er,
And saw amongst the scorched and uptorn grass
A shapeless, black, and incoherent mass.
 The tree was one huge cinder ; from it broke,
  With suffocating stench and threatening flare,
 Up to the sky, a pillar of thick smoke,
  Which wreathed around and clouded all the
  air.


### XXXIX.

While they stood, dumbly wondering at the
 sight
Of death and horror, onward came the white
And woe-worn Emily—with vacant face
That loathsome lump she hastened to embrace,
 And pressed it to her bosom, and then hid
  Her soft cheek under it, and, madly gay,
 She called it love, and with quick accent chid
  The lifeless matter for its voiceless play.

### XL.

She cast some fading blossoms on the spot,
And muttered words which ears receivèd not ;
Her eyes were fixed upon the empty air,
And at some well-known face appeared to stare.
   But recollection struck her, and she threw
     A woeful glance upon the awe-struck group,
   And, with a noiseless footstep, onward flew
     Into the woods, with a discordant whoop.

### XLI.

They bore the wreck of Albert to a grave
O'er which the graceful willows sadly wave,
And with their dewy tears each evening weep
Upon the lovely form that lies asleep.
   But she, sad wanderer, amidst the grove
     Built a poor bower, and laid her throbbing
       head
   Upon the grave, calling upon her love,
     All motionless and ghastly as the dead.

### XLII.

In the bright summer evenings she would lie
Basking in light, and with a melting eye
Look for her Albert, welcoming the air,
Thinking she felt his spirit glowing there ;
   Then to the light caresses of the wind
     She bared her breast, and pouted lips to kiss
   The downy breeze; it pleased her mourning
       mind ;
     So would she wanton in her simple bliss.

### XLIII.

Thus lived she all her summer months away,
In useless wailings and fantastic play :
No noxious thing crawled near her loveliness ;
The little birds too pitied her distress,
   And sung to her, and innocently crept,
     To her warm bosom.  In a narrow way
A hind benighted, whilst all others slept,
     Saw 'midst the trees her face, and heard
       her lay.

### EMILY'S PLAINT.

Oh ! why art thou gone, love ?
   Oh ! why art thou gone ?
Thou hast left me alone, love,
   Broken-hearted, alone.

My heart is grief-frozen,
   My bosom's in pain ;
Dost thou wish, love, to cure it ?
   Oh come back again.

Thou swor'st, a fond lover,
   Here ever to stay ;
Three months are past over,
   Yet still thou'rt away.

I've pulled thee some flowers,
   I've spread thee some heath,
I'll deck thee, return'd, with
   A rosy-red wreath.

But, ah ! the wind whispers,
  The murmuring wind,
" Thine Albert is dead, and
  Has left thee behind."


Return for an instant,
  Mine Albert, I pray,
And lap me in glory
  And bear me away.


## XLIV.

In autumn she grew speechless ; no light shone
In her dead eye, her memory was gone.
Some of the peasants fed her, like a tame
And hungry robin, every day she came
  To the kind hand that gave her food ; at last
    She kissed it timidly, and gently smiled ;
  A quivering tear across her paleness passed,
    And she sobbed dumbly, like a voiceless
      child.


## XLV.

One chill September morning she was found
Silently kneeling on her lover's mound ;
The passers thought she slept, but when they tried,
Her lifted hands fell coldly by her side.
  Her eyelids were half closed, her bloodless pair
    Of open lips seemed gratefully to bless,
  As if stern death had heard her simple prayer,
    And kissed her beauty into stoniness.

### XLVI.

They laid her underneath the self-same grass,
In her dead Albert's bosom ; they who pass,
In summer evenings, hear unearthly sighs,
Dazzled by glimpses of concealèd eyes.
  A thornless rose and lily mark the grave,
    That grew spontaneous from the buried pair,
  And ever, while in zephyr's sighs they wave,
    A downy perfume whispers in the air.

# THE INDUCTION
## TO THE SECOND FYTTE.

THE minstrel ceased ; the music's wings
Swept lingering through the bounding
    strings ;
  With parting kiss his fingers brushed
The startled lyre, and all was hushed.
Again the feasters sang and laughed,
Again the beaded wine was quaffed.
The youth retired alone, unseen,
To wander o'er the fringy green
Of moonlight meadows, and to gaze
Upon the water-mirrored rays
Of stars, that sable midnight crown,
Like radiant blessings peeping down
From heaven upon our slumbers.   There
He found the solitary fair
Agnes, in pensive mood reclined,
Feasting with dreams her thoughtful mind ;
Light from her eyelids seemed to soar,
Her beauteous cheeks lay clustered o'er
With curling tufts of amber thread
That twined around her pillowed head,

Like some plump peach, in sweetness ripe,
Spangled with many a dewy stripe,
Courted and kissed by every breeze,
Just severed from the parent trees,
That sleeps transparent grapes among,
On waving tendrils thickly strung.
At his approach she rose awhile,
And becked him onward with a smile,
In which her soul looked forth.   "Once more,"
She cried, "a tale of fairy lore:
Sing, minstrel boy, of them who stray
In rainbow livery by day,
And nightly sleep in closing breast
Of summer flowers ; or those that, dressed
In robes of flame, 'mongst marshes dance,
And dazzle with a wavering glance
The frightened clown ; or those who creep
Under our eyelids whilst we sleep,
And dally with our thoughts : thou know'st
Full many a tale of shrieking ghost,
And wandering fay, and gibing sprite,
That laugh away the hours of night."
Her words flew gently from her tongue,
Like bees whose wings are honey-clung,
Bubbling through sweetness.   As she said,
The youthful songster waved his head,
And summoned music from its sleep
Among the chords ; with murmur deep,
And faltering accent, thus he sung,
Whilst his hand roved the strings among ;
And she, with eyelash downward cast,
Caught his wild story from the blast.

# RODOLPH.

### I.

THERE is a massy cloud of dismal hue
Climbing reluctantly the pathless blue ;
It is the pall of the departed day ;
And, after it, the self-same silent way,
A heavy troop of mist-clad mourners wend,
And down the lampless, dim horizon bend :
   The grave and cradle of short-livèd time,
     Ocean, receives them with its gaping billows,
   And with the hóarse notes, which its death-song
      chime,
   Lulls on its breast the infant day it pillows.

### II.

Then Twilight, the dank ghost of murdered hours,
Creeps with still, clammy pace around the bowers,
Summoning from its rest the drowsy owl,
And listening cheerlessly to wolfish howl,
Rocking its wan, chill spirit on the cloud,
And weeping dew-drops to the wailings loud
   Of the consoling blast ; and mournfully
     Baring to earth its breathless, fog-veil'd breast,
   Declaring how the nameless moments die
     Of the red wound, that blushes in the west.

### III.

But on their best-loved flowers, that perished brood,
Cast their last kiss of perfume and of blood,
Tinge with their dying breath some opening bloom,
And breathe one sigh, then hurry to their tomb.

Thence the broad rose in velvet bed of moss,
And pink-fringed daisy with its golden boss,
  The chequer-leaved carnation, plump-cheeked
     pip
   Of bristling holly, 'mongst its armèd leaves,
  Borrow their crimson richness, and the lip
   Of innocence in infant sleep that heaves.

### IV.

There was a calm of sleep among the hills,
The whispering zephyrs chid the brawling rills.
It was a time for musing ; every gale
In murmurs seemed to syllable a tale
To the mute flowers, which bent their buds to hear,
While evening lent their closing eyes a tear.
  It was a place for lovers' gentle plaint,
    Afar from glittering show and boisterous halls,
  Where, from her bower of blossoms, Echo faint
    Attuned her voice to bubbling waterfalls.

### V.

A silent lake, the mirror of the night,
There lashed in mimic rage and playful spite
Its lily-fringèd banks, and, gaily bold,
Crowned its dwarf billows with the moonlight gold,
Casting around its spray in pearly showers,
A soft bequest to all the thirsting flowers.
  Upon the couch of moss, a lovelorn wight
    Sate, calmly listening to the tittering breeze,
  Then tuned his lyre, and roused, with finger light,
    The sleeping strings, and sang such words as
      these :

## THE MADRIGAL.

How sweet is the voice of the beauty I love,
    As the violet's scent at eventide ;
As the first, softest sigh of the nestling dove,
    As the laughter of fairies when they ride.
      As soft as the evening breeze,
        As sweet as the blackbird's song,
      As gentle as summer bees
        That flutter the garden among.

But oh ! when she chides with her beautiful lips,
    'Tis like the gay butterfly's playful spite,
Which peevishly spurns the fair blossom he sips,
    Trampling its sweetness with all his weak might.
      As loud as the angry showers,
        As harsh as the zephyr of May,
      As dark as the noon-day bowers,
        As bright as the glowworm's ray.

She warbles : 'tis the cheerful lark that sings,
    Bidding good day to the new-risen light ;
'Tis the sound of the hymning angels' wings,
    Rustling 'mid the sunbeams in their flight.
      As lovely as bees' sweet tune,
        That ever in honey is dipped ;
      As tender as cowslips in June,
        Ere the dewdrops from them dripped.

Ay me ! when she timidly hinted her truth,
    It fell and it lightened my heart with love,
Like the busy whisper of morn in its youth,
    That tells of the beauties and glories above.

As pure as the evening dew,
    That sleeps in the folded flowers ;
And as clear as the heavenly blue,
    Which shines on the noon-day hours.


### VI.

He ceased.   And was it Echo, that poured round
So sweet, so sad, so musical a sound,
Winding around his sense with fainting note,
Like closing circles in a parted moat?
It cannot be : again are borne along
The whispered burthens of a distant song.
   There seemed an hundred voices flying nigh,
     Bearing their sweetness to his strainèd ear ;
   At length the flowrets, with a scented sigh,
     Tremblingly echoed, " Follow, follow, Dear ;
      Follow, follow, follow,
       Over mount and over hollow,
        Follow."


### VII.

'Twas like the sounds we dream of.   Such a call
Summons the spirit from its earthen hall
When smiling infants die ; it sunk and rose
In tuneful wavelets, lulling to repose
Suspicious fear ; it rocked upon the wind
Awhile, then fled and left a scent behind.
   Rodolph sprang up ; it was not Anna's song,
     Who bade him stay ; it had attractive force :
   Forgetting her, who made him wait so long,
     He rushed to trace the music to its source.

## VIII.

Then from the lake was heard a sudden sigh ;
Straightway the sportive billows arched on high,
And from the flower-strewn bed of the calm stream
Up shot a fiery pillar, like the beam
Of love which lightens through the slender veil
Of maiden, listening to a lover's tale.
  A ball of fire rose through the yawning stream,
    Spouting its fevered venom with a roar,
  Whirling around the lake its lurid gleam,
    And snowing its red light upon the shore.

## IX.

The kindled water, with a foaming rush,
Strove its defying foe at once to crush ;
The flame spurned the huge billows with a gnash
Of curlèd flame, and water-spouting dash,
And struggled onward with a piercing wind,
Leaving a deep and steaming scar behind.
  It reached the surface: and a red canoe
    Of flickering brightness, with a motion fleet,
  Seemed the recoiling water to pursue,
    And brustled fiercely up to Rodolph's feet.

## X.

It stopped upon the bank, a ball of glare :
Ring within ring of tinted flame was there,
And from the midst an eye-like violet spark
Fearfully glimmered through the murky dark.
About the outer ring of livid flame
A swarm of quivering sparklets went and came,

Like fiery bees, whilst hollow murmurings,
   And the hoarse lispings of the muttering light,
Spake nourishment; they, with their darting
      wings,
   Seared the dew-cherished turf and flowers
   bright.

### XI.

From out the dingy smoke,—which slowly wound,
Hissing, in serpent folds along the ground,—
A fiery hand appeared, and beckoning slow,
With waving fingers urged the youth to go.
Meanwhile his sense was charmèd with a song,
That drew him, with the clue of sound, along.
   The rippling lake was hushed, as if each nymph,
     To catch those notes of chaunted melody,
   Were pillowed softly on her couch of lymph,
     Or 'twere the saucy wavelets' lullaby.

### THE SONG.

Hither haste, and gently strew
His velvet path with odorous dew
   Which slept on roses' cheeks a night;
Stud the turf with the golden flower
In which the glowworm builds its bower,
   And gladdens with its tender light.
Sprinkle here the twinkling shower
On each perfume-stifled flower.

Hither haste, and gently fling
All the opening buds of spring;
   And, if a drooping leaf appear,

Tinge it with this coloured roll
Which I from the rainbow stole,
  And hang a spangle on its ear.
Sprinkle here the twinkling shower
On each perfume-stifled flower.

Hither haste with daffodils,
That court the glass of gliding rills,
  And violets with their blue veils o'er,
And the king-cup, in whose bell
The thief of honey loves to dwell,
  And paints it with his yellow store.
Sprinkle here the twinkling shower,
On each perfumê-stifled flower.

### THE CHANGE.

They are waiting for you,
    Whose forms you ne'er saw ;
Their eyes dimmed with dew,
    The warm sigh they draw.
Then follow, follow, follow ;
Over bank and over hollow
Still with fearless footstep follow.

### XII.

Silence engulph'd the words.   The waving hand,
Still beckoning from the mist, flamed its command;
And, with clear sparks that wandered from the
       mass,
In burning lines traced " Follow " on the grass.
Rodolph waved onward, and the silent guide
Passed on before with bounding leaps and wide ;

And as he stepped, fresh buds bloomed at his
    feet,
  And tiny voices whispered in his ear,
Whilst fragrant gales wept music, him to greet,
  And all was sweetness he could see or hear.

### XIII.

Still on and on the scorching leader flew,
And, where it leaped, startled the sleeping dew ;
Putting on varied forms the time to while,
And passing gaily many a dreary mile :
Now as a dog it scoured along the vale,
With winking eye of blue and smoky tail ;
  Now like a mazy serpent creeping through
    The piercing briars, twisted from the light,
  Its twining body all a changeful hue,
    Its venomed jaws with sparkling fury white.

### XIV.

When on the hillocks they began to roam,
It darted down a cataract of foam,
With dancing spray and bubbles of red blaze
Chasing each other through the bickering maze.
Still on they went—o'er plains, o'er vale, o'er
    knoll ;
At length the wheeling splendour ceased to roll,
  And pointed onward to a low-browed cave ;
    Then sprung up from the ground with chirrup
      gay,
  And, like a fire-winged lark, hastened to wave
    Its plumes, and bounded on its airy way.

### XV.

It was upon a turfy mound, below
A brook was glittering with pallid glow,
And the cave's arch was bowered o'er with stems
That nodded gently, laden with bright gems ;
Whilst from within came notes of melody,
Now sad, now gay, and chased each other by :
  And, fleeting with the mazes of the tune,
    Soared words alight with tenderness and love,
  Like the coy beams of the reluctant moon,
    Struggling in winged embrace of clouds above.


### XVI.

That chaunt was sweet as bubbling notes that
        spring
From smooth, deep founts, and faint into a ring,
The love-sick sighs of water-nymph unseen,
Toying with broad-leaved weeds so rich with green:
It welcomed him, and seemed his steps to invite
From the unseemly mist of clammy night.
  He entered with expectant, glad amaze,
    And soon he found that narrow lane of moss
  Led to a hall, built up of crystal blaze,
    And softened all around with silken gloss.


### XVII.

Against the walls fresh-blooming jasmine twined,
Unscorched by heat, unblasted by the wind ;
And through its curling tendrils incense flew,
Kissing in wavy clouds the bosomed dew,
Or streaming faintly in the amorous air,
Like the light, tangled locks of ladies' hair.

Through silken curtains, gently curved below,
   Stilly crept moonlight beams; so glittering
      weeds
Peep through the cloudy waters where they grow,
   Among the fickle sands and pebble beads.

## XVIII.

Deep in the leaves of mossy-bedded posies
Of sickly lilies, violets, and roses,
Nestled bright balls of amber radiance,
Which cast on all the shrubs a starry glance;
Like the bright silkworm, which its cradle weaves
Unseen amongst the mulberry's curlèd leaves:
   And on the down-lined leaflet's inside moss
      Drooped lengthened tears of crystal, quivering
        studs
   Of melted light;—around they poured their gloss,
      And dyed, with mimic rainbows, all the buds.

## XIX.

Up at the further end, 'mid spicy wine,
Breathing the odour of its parent vine,
Were toying maids, some joining their fair faces
In rosy garlands, beating measured paces;
Some pelting one another in their mirth
With glistening leaves, which wavered to the
      earth.
   Some on curved arms and softly drooping head
      Mused with closed lips and fringy curtained
        eyes
   Among the upward flowers, as though they read
      Some bee-graven song, or heard the blossoms'
        sighs.

### XX.

'Upon a velvet couch of mossy rings,
Enamelled o'er with bud-like glitterings,
Sate she who seemed the mistress ; round her
   played
A maiden band, which all her signs obeyed.
The startled youth she beckoned silently,
Who waded through the flood of harmony
   Up to her side ; she motioned him to sit,
      But nothing spoke. The mossy throne he
         pressed,
   While from her looks keen arrows seemed to flit,
      And pierce with lovely cruelty his breast.

### XXI.

Her eyes were rooted on the shepherd boy,
And in their depth of blue swam love and joy :
Her mouth !—Oh pardon me, thou coral cave,
Prison of fluttering sighs, cradle and grave
Of noiseless kisses, if I fail to tell
The beauty and the grace that in thee dwell.
   'Twas like a pouting, dew-bespangled flower,
      Breathing deliciousness ; her slender tongue
   A babbling bee in it, with all his power,
      Murmuring the sweetness forth which round
         him clung.

### XXII.

Then sweetly she began those lips to move,
And whispered in his ear a lay of love.
Her words were drops of music ; as they swept,
Clammy with odour, folds of softness crept

Snakily round his soul ; he tried to brush
Off from her lips that love-enamelled flush ;
  She stayed him gently, " First, loved Rudolph,
     swear
    To be mine only," smilingly she said.
"I vow!" he cried, "and let me seal it there."—
  At those words, lightning-like, the vision fled.


### XXIII.

His ears were stunned by an hoarse, fiendish roar
Of laughter ; he fell leaden on the floor,
And all had vanished.—It was dark and cold ;
A putrid steam rose from the clammy mould :
The moon darts through a crevice ; at his lips
He sees a skull's mouth yawn, which thickly drips
  With nauseous moisture ; upward to his thigh
    He stood in bones and dust of bodies dead ;
  And part was newly melting, part was dry,
    And part, with recent slaughter, glaring red.


### XXIV.

He waded onward, and the wingèd dust
Flew up and choaked him, the dry, skinny crust
Cracked at his steps ; the bones with feeble crash
Bent under him, and many a steaming splash
Of melting flesh showered on him as he stood ;
The track was slippery with spouting blood.
  Fitfully through a distant, narrow chink
    The dismal light crawled in : he saw below
  A body-jammèd vault with yawning brink ;
    He felt the breath of death against his temples
    glow.

### XXV.

Just at his feet a grinning skeleton
Stretched its worm-twinèd arms of chalky bone,
And rattled its thin finger in the blast ;
Its spikèd teeth were dumbly chattering fast,
As if its death-dream were disturbed ; by him
Another lay with yawning jawbone grim,
   Through which the cold wind whistled ; down
      its cheek
     Crept death's chill sweat.   Rodolph essayed
      to pass,
   But fear chained down his strength ; with strug-
     gles weak
     He plunged among the death-cemented mass.

### XXVI.

At length he heard some yawning, muttered
      groans,
And feeble shufflings of the brittle bones,
As if the bodies rose to welcome him ;
Athwart his eyes dark shadows seemed to swim,
And leave a death-kiss there.   A moist hand soon
Pressed into his, and by the shivering moon
  He saw his welcomer, the ribs that kept
    No prisoned heart within their crumbled bars,
  And to his eyeless sockets fat worms crept,
    Whose eyes peeped out like lurid meteor stars.

### XXVII.

He closed his eyes, but still that shape was
     there,
Mocking his agony with lifeless glare.

Rodolph held up his fever-parchèd hands,
And twined his head round in those swollen
    bands;
He clutched his hair, all clotted with fear's dew,
And crusted with the choaking dust that flew:
  He sank down heavily amid the heap,
    And felt the worms come, coldly nibbling
  His tottering limbs; then down came leaden
    sleep,
And struck him into slumber with its wing.


XXVIII.

Day passed, and day; no Rodolph tuned at eve
The twilight pipe, that taught the woods to grieve;
Morning and noon the shepherd's hue and cry
Roused the dim echo on the mountains high.
The sabbath came.  And with the early morn
The sexton rose the chancel to adorn,
  And wake the sleeping bells; he walked along
    Close by the charnel-house; there came a
    sound
  Of grating laughter mixed with ribald song,
    As though the dead were 'wakened in the
    ground.


XXIX.

With trembling hand he fitted the old key
In the nail-studded door; his straining knee
Forced back its rust-tuned hinge; with fearful
    wink
He peeped within through a decaying chink,
And saw the madman playing, like a child,
With the foul carcase-crumbs around him piled:

I.                                  Q

He tossed the bones about, and whispered low
  With bloodless lips ; and with the struggling
     snakes
And jaggèd splinters fashioned round his brow
  A garland, gemmèd o'er with bloody flakes..


### XXX.

The dreading pauper flew, and left alone
That sad and thoughtless man to his wild moan,
Who crawled out from his dungeon, and his days
Lurked out amongst the woods and untrod ways.
He sate among the tombs and called the dead
With voice familiar ; and by some 'tis said
  He ate forbidden food : the leper toad,
    The screeching owl, and the rank carrion crow,
  Tamely frequented his obscure abode,
    And slept together in his bosom low.


### XXXI.

He sometimes howled at the bright moon ; forgot
The power of speech, and o'er his cheek a blot
Of melancholy black was spread ; he knew
Where berried night-shade and hoar hemlock
     grew,
And made his bower of them : the beldames blind,
The wrinkled crones, heard on the midnight wind
  His raving whoops, and shuddered o'er their
    fire,
    Telling the tale : he laughed in madness too
  When the loud thunder rolled, and cloud-clad
    choir
    Of sweeping winds in the dank midnight blew,

### XXXII.

At last, upon a twilight eve, he stole
Into the village.   Under a dark knoll
Of elms there was an old moss-cushioned seat,
O'er which he'd scrambled with his infant feet;
He dropped upon it gently.   A huge tear
Swept his stern features at that prospect dear,
   Still he said nothing.   But the children crept
      With terror from their sports, and, lisping, told
   Of the dread comer; the next one who stepped
      Up to the hillock found him dead and cold.

## THE INDUCTION
## TO THE THIRD FYTTE.

THE tale was said. Fair Agnes rose,
And tripped to court a night's repose ;
There in her chamber soon she lay,
(Her every dream with warblings gay
Of fairies serenaded,) hidden
'Midst folds of warmth, while night-clouds, ridden
By thought-winged visions, and bright fringed
With rosy thoughts, her slumbers tinged ;
Like bashful fragrance, buried deep
In curling leaves, that nightly weep
Their melted souls of sweets away.
The minstrel turned : a feeble ray
Of quivering came slowly nigh,
And ancient Margaret caught his eye.
She was an old and tottering crone ;
Her skin was shrivelled round the bone,
And seemed a sear-cloth wrapped around
A 'wakened mummy. O'er the ground
Her feet were wandering doubtfully ;
And in her stagnant, frozen eye,
The last blue spark was glimmering.

The years behind had stayed to fling
The silver crown of reverend age,—
The halo that adorns the sage,—
Upon her thinly sprinkled curls,
That grew, like vegetable pearls
Of mistletoe, around her brow,
And bounded on her temples low.
Her voice came stumbling o'er her teeth,
Half frozen by her misty breath,
Chaining the ear with broken links
Of muttered words.   With joyful winks,
And shivering hands, that tried to clasp
The songster in their feeble grasp,
She hailed the youth, and drew his arm
Into her own, while to a warm
Small room she led him ; there she placed
All that is sweet to sight or taste.
The wine, that rolled in sunny tears
In gold-lined cups with massive ears ;
While from the bright depth quickly spring
Bubbles in many a bounding string,
Like golden eggs with sweetness swelling,
Whence, on the surface gently dwelling,
On steamy wing of brightness rushes
The halcyon of those sparkling gushes,
Pleasure, hatched beneath the bowl,
That warbles rapture to the soul.
The while he drank, she praised his power,
And bribed his presence for an hour ;
A lay of wildness loud he sung,
While the old dame in silence hung
Upon the marvels of his tongue.

## LEOPOLD.

### I.

THE battle is over ; the dews of the fog
The wings of the eager vultures clog ;
And the souls of the dead, in many a flake,
Are winding aloft, a misty snake
From its blood-clotted lair with fresh slaughter
   tinged :
And the clouds of heaven, with sable fringed,
Are weeping the murder : the spirit of ill
Is snuffing the incense upon the hill,
And basking with joy in the mortal steam,
And dabbling in the blood-red stream.
The tempest is moistening its blast in the blood
Which trickles along in a scurfy flood.
The dead are all reeking, a ghastly heap,
Slippery with gore, and with crushed bones
   steep ;
As if the flesh had been snowed on the hills,
And dribbled away in blood-clammy rills :
A swamp of distorted faces it lay,
And sweltered and bubbled in the broad day.
There was one who had fainted in battle's crash,
Now he struggled in vain with feeble splash
Under his warm tomb of motionless dead ;
At last he dashed backward his bursting head,
And gasped in his hideous agony,
And ground his firm teeth, and darted his eye ;
Then wriggled his lips in the last prayer of death,
And mixed with the whirlwind his foamed
   breath.

Another, with gold-hilted sabre girt,
Had crawled from amid the fermenting dirt,
And was creeping with torture along the ground,
Tracking his path with an opening wound ;
But a plunderer, spying his failing form,
Scattered his brains as hot food for the storm.
Hard by was a smiling young infant at rest
On his death-frozen mother's chilly breast,
And he filled her deaf ears with his piteous cries ;
And with tiny fingers opened her eyes,
Which spurted upon him a thick, gory clot,
While he smiled and fingered the spreading blot.
Amongst the foul carcases slowly there went
A reverend hermit, weak and bent,
Muttering prayers with a tremulous tongue,
Whilst groans of despair at his deafened ears
      hung.
As he slipped on the dead men they started and
      howled,
And the lapping dogs stirred not but angrily
      growled.
A carrion crow, that was whetting its bill
On a naked bone, which was reeking still,
Heavily flapped its broad wings for a flight,
But could not soar upward, so gorged all night.

## II.

The holy man raised up the smiling boy,
Who laughed, and held his blood-tinged fingers up;
His lip was moist, as though he'd made a cup
Out of some foaming wound : he turned and cried,
And struggled from the gentle father's side,
And played with the torn flesh as with a toy.

His kind preserver, with some pious verse,
Hymned him to sleep within his arms; the child
Breathed balmily, and in his vision smiled.
And there he lay, swathed in that hallowed rest,
Like a late blossom pillowed on the breast
Of shrivelled leaves, as on an early hearse.
The hermit was old father Hubert; he
Who dwelt alone upon the pathless hill,
The friend of man in action and in will;
From whose soft eye, beneath the silver crown
Of age, beamed a pure sprite, like fresh rain, down
Upon the weak and suffering.  If there be,
As we will hope there is, benevolence,
And love of men and heaven, and charity,
That pours libations from the balmy eye,
Left in the world, his heart was the pure shrine
Of all that's beauteous, kindly, and divine.
And so his words came, as the holy scents
From altar in prayer-echoing recess,
Steaming with clemency and holiness.
He was a man would make us love mankind,
Though all the rest were worms as vile as blind.


### III.

With joy, that winged his feet, kind Hubert bore
His blooming burthen onward to his cell,
A rock-walled tower, alone within the dell,
Which beaded ivy bowered, and a bright stream
Girdled, besprinkled with the sun's bright beam,
As though 'twas tracked by the golden oar
Of unseen voy'ger; on its banks there smiled
All plants of sweetness; the prim daisy, and
The studded cowslip on its slender wand,

Like a small, natural sceptre; violets too,
Dark coloured, seemed the passer's smile to woo;
And leaf-veiled lilies of the valley, wild,
Shunning the others, like a froward child:
They mottled variously old Hubert's path,
And seemed to know his footstep, for they cast
Up their soft cups and quivered as he passed.
He loved them as his children, innocent
And sweet, and guiltless of unkind intent;
He moistened them when the breath-scorching
    dawn
Denied them dew: of these he plucked a set,
The freshest and the fairest, and most wet,
And strewed them plentifully on a nest
Of moss, and laid the baby to its rest.

### IV.

Oh it is sweet to watch o'er innocence
Asleep, and mark the calm breast fall and rise,
And the veined veils that casket up the eyes,
And smiles dimple the cheek, for then we know
Good thoughts sweep by upon the gales that
    blow.—
Hubert brought up in his benevolence
The orphan child, and called him Leopold:
It was a froward babe, and never laughed,
Nor stole a kiss by courtesy or craft,
Nor with its out-stretched arms his bosom clipped,
Nor in the evening blithely round him tripped.
Its eye was leaden, motionless, and cold;
It skulked in corners, and shunned sulkily
The good man's lessons; never conned a word
Of prayer or holiness.   He oft was heard,

When all was silent save the midnight wind,
Muttering the secret thoughts of his dark mind;
But lowering fled from the monk's rosary,
And howled to drown his morning hymn of joy.
So he grew on, this sullen, wayward boy,
Chaining his dismal thoughts in their birth-place,
A blotting cloud in Hubert's heaven of grace.


### v.

He knew no playmates but the stormy blasts,
Which seemed to whisper some dark secret dread
As he would sleep among them, with his head
Swathed in lank dripping tresses, and cry out
With joy to his rude playmates, while his shout
(He thought) was written in the lightning red.
Oh ! how he longed to bind his bronzed brows
With a bright snake of fire, wove from the flame
Of those swift glimpses ; or to hear his name
Roared in the thunder which they gild : he raged
And bared his breast, wherein were cribbed and
     caged
The thoughts that seared it. Then with mops
     and mows
He darted through the storm, like some wild bird :
He spurned the wind, and stretched his longing
     arms,
Hugging the tempest and its brood of harms
With horrible delight ; his whooping yell
Struggled with the hoarse blast ; its striving swell
Dwelt on the clouds, and in the vales was heard.
His bursting veins seemed swollen with venomed
     fire ;
His eye was ringed with lurid flashiness,

And to his leaping heart he seemed to press
Some fanged folded thing of fieriness;
His lips, he felt, foamed lava, and his hair,
A cluster of writhed fire-snakes, to the air
Spat out the lightnings of its scorn and ire.
After such maddest fits his eye was sunk
Deep in its socket, and his lifeless trunk
Lay, like a lump of clay, amid the rank,
Long, twisted grass that decked his chosen bank.
And, as he lay entranced, the silent breeze
Swept from his foam-bathed lips such words as
     these :

## VI.

" Ye swiftly flitting hours of day and night,
Half dim and dusk, half sunny bright,
Like feathers moulting from the pied wing
Of breathless time, who flutters evermore,
This ball of earth and ocean girdling,
Searching the crevices of sea and shore,
Which still defy his strength with billowy roar,
To spy some cranny which the light ne'er saw,
Chaotic and forgotten, wherein he
May 'scape the gulp of the sepulchral jaw
       Of loitering Eternity.
Our lives still fall and fall, flake upon flake,
  Like piling snow upon the waves
      Of some vast lake,
  And melt away into the caves,
Whilst rising bubbles waste them as they break,
Like ye, from our own substance; as ye pass
Our essence still ye pilfer, onward fleeing;
We vanish, as a thing that never was,

And become drops of the huge ever-being.
Oh tell me, if ye silent wisdom bring,—
Ye smallest links of time's unravelled chain,
That join to buried first the unborn last,
The embryo future to the sunken past,—
Tell me, (for ye have not been forged in vain,
And ye have seen the fountain whence we spring,)
What is this life, that spins so strangely on
That, ere we grasp and feel it, it is gone?
Is it a vision? Are we sleeping now
In the sweet sunshine of another world?
Is all that seems but a sleep-conjured ghost,
And are our blindfold senses closely curled,
Our powerful minds pent up in this frail brow
But by our truant fancy? Are we a groping host
Of sleepers gazing in this twilight gleam,
Unconscious dupes of some thought-peopled dream?
But I will think no more, lest haply I,
If I erred on in thought's dim wilderness,
And scared myself with shadows, ne'er should die,
But my astounded soul might petrify
And freeze into time-scoffing stoniness."

## VII.

There would he lie, aye; and there was a cave,
Hideous and dark, choked up with thorny weeds,
Moss-shrouded, that ne'er cast around their seeds;
And the dew lay among them, where it fell,
For months and months, and then it 'gan to swell
And turned to poison, where they still would wave
Inward; where tangled knots of loathsome roots
Crept, webbed, on the roof. The dusk recess
Was moistened o'er with drops of clamminess;

And, 'mid rank bunches of envenomed shrubs,
Glittering with serpents' lathered foam, and grubs
Naked and filthy crawling on the shoots,
A stagnant well steamed out dense, stifling mists,
Whose brim was silvered with the slimy track
Of tardy snails, or toads with mottled back,
Which hundred years hatched in the chilly stone.
Around the fog-filled cave no wind was blown,
Save pantings of huge snakes, bedded in twists
Of purple nightshade, and rough hemlock's hair.
The very owls fled, screeching, from the den,
And leathern bats were stifled there.   No men
Ever set foot there till mad Leopold came
And sucked the water in, to quench his flame.
Well for its murkiness he loved the lair.
There, breathless, would he stretch his limbs among
The hideous crawlers ; feel the forked tongue
Of crested serpents tamely lick his hand,
And curl around his legs with sparkling band.
There would he mark discoloured damps, that crept
Cloggedly down, and listen to the sound
Of the huge drops that pattered on the ground
From the damp, mouldy clay, and see dark shapes
Mock his deep thoughts with gibes and fiery gapes,
Whole days unmoved, until his spirit slept.

### VIII.

One wretched day (he had been sleeping long)
He started from his slumber, roused again
By some sharp pang of intellectual pain ;
He cast with fevered balls a shuddering glance
Upon his couch, and, eager to advance,
Trampled the torpid snakes he slept among,

That lashed their slimy tails, when from the gloom
Of yellow chilliness that brooded o'er
The well in clouds, and swept along the floor,
Hatching parched blasts of poison, there up-wound
To him an indistinct, word-shaping sound,
Breathing the clammy vapour of the tomb;
It crept into his ears, and bound him there,
As though by spell-sprung roots, and thus it spake:
" Dost thou, oh human reptile, seek to slake
Thy thirst of power; to ride along the deep,
And dally with the lightning, and to sleep
Under the tempest's wing, robed in the flare
Of the fierce thunder-bolt?  Answer, weak slave."
" I do, I do," he cried, with struggling voice.
" The thunder hears, and doth approve thy choice.
All shalt thou earn by the priest Hubert's death.
Mix with the wind this night his feeble breath,
And cast his blood into yon green-scummed wave."
The voice was gone, the echoes all were hushed,
And, by some fiend impelled, on Leopold rushed;
He scoured along the plain, the streams he passed
Breathless, and entered Hubert's cell at last.

### IX.

He entered.   The old man was sleeping; prayer
Steamed murmuring from his lips; a mouldered cross,
Which the moon gilt, rose on a mossy boss
Behind his pallet, strewn with leafy wreaths,
O'er which the mellow autumn colour breathes;
A swinging lamp lit up with fitful flare
The dingy cave, now grasping at the air
With upstretched claw of fire, now sinking down,
And quivering in blue atoms.   Leopold stood

And gazed upon the slumber of the good.
Tranced Hubert's soul was dallying with dreams
Flowery and pure, that wander on the beams
Of the moon earthward, with the night-breeze blown
Into the ears of sleepers. "Darling child,"
The old man uttered, waking, "art thou here
Again to please me?" With a guilty fear
All Leopold's limbs grew stiff: the fading spark
Expired, and left the cavern damp and dark;
And then a spirit blasted in his ear,
With syllables of fire, the unnamed deed,
The sentence of the hermit. 'Twas decreed.
The dagger trembled in the ingrate's grasp;
It fell; he heard his friend's last struggling gasp,
And felt the blood-stream bubbling warmly round
His fingers, and drop down with gushing sound;
He heard the echo startle at the groans
Half choaked with feebleness; those faltered
      moans
Muttered his name with blessings. Then he fled,
And left his friend and kind preserver dead.

### X.

He plunged the blushing dagger in the well
Of stagnant filth, which foamed up hideous din
And grating laughter at the acted sin:
Then Leopold felt his heels winged with flame,
And scorching breezes quickly went and came,
Feathering his limbs with sparks. The earth all fell
Diminishing below him, while he strode
Among the winking stars; as there he stayed
To taste the torrents that around him played,
Athwart his path the steed of tempest passed,

Its nostrils foaming with the whirlwind blast;
And as it stumbled, with hoofs comet-shod,
Among the craggy clouds, forked lightning's spark
Tracked through the midnight its destructive course,
Whilst from his wind-lulled cave the thunder hoarse
Echoed its snortings.  The blind nightmare too,
Crawling upon a cloud of murky hue,
Strolled lazily along, ridden by dark
And grinning phantoms.  Still he wandered on
Among the elements: he lay by night
Under the tempest's wing, where fogs and blight
Are cradled, or a messenger from death
Flew down with feverish dreams and sucked the
       breath
Out of parched lips until the soul was gone.
Thus centuries were passed.  One night of fog,
When winter with his damps began to clog
The pestilential air, he issued forth
Upon a mist-winged frost, and came to earth.


### XI.

Oh woman ! flower among this wilderness
Of wickedness and woe, whose soul of love
Lies scent-like inmost, steaming out above
Its incense of soft words; how sweet to sip
Entranced the voice of rapture from thy lip,
And taste thy soul in kisses.  Thou dost bless
Our earthly life with looks, and shinest afar,
Gilding our night of misery like the star
That beams with hope upon the mariner:
Our guardian angels, robed in lovely clouds,
Ye still attend our steps in smiling crowds,—
Friends, mothers, sisters, comforters, and wives.

Darkness and sorrow blot our lonely lives
When we forget or spurn ye. If ye err,
Justice should weep but frown not. Lovely voice
Of angels, caught and cagèd in a place
Hallowed by pity, tenderness, and grace,
Echo of every better, softer thought
That man is blessed with. Vain the solace sought
From wine, that bubbles with disease and steams
With embryo riot; thine, oh thine alone
Are the soft moments, when our souls have flown
From out this crust of flesh, and tremblingly
Hang on our lips, and vainly strive to fly
On pinions of bright words, and join with thine.
Oh that the magic skill of verse were mine
For one brief moment, that in lines of gold
Thy truth might be embalmed ! But I am bold,
And worthier spirits have embowered thy shrine
In wreaths of poesy, with scents that glow.—
So briefly to our tale of guilt and woe.

### XII.

He came to earth.—It was a hamlet rude
He entered ; in the midst a building stood
Embraced by creeping plants, which murmered low
Their voice of sweetness to the evening shower.
One little casement in that humble bower
Pressed out its chequered lattice in the leaves,
And kissed them into varied blushes. Sheaves
Of buds stood bristling up ; in many a row
Curving laburnum wept its golden tears
Of perfume, and the saucy jasmine tossed
Its puny blossom and its curled leaf glossed
With narrow green : they all appeared to peep

I.                                                    R

In silent joy on some fair thing asleep.
Then Leopold on his dusty charger rears
Himself among the shuddering boughs.    What
    sight
Lay melting on that snowy couch of white?—
A beauteous daughter of mankind.    Her cheek
Bloomed through ethereal dust, that veiled its bliss
From the down-falling light and night-wind's kiss.—
He saw—he saw and loved.    Next night again
He came, but viewed the beauty racked with pain.

## XIII.

\*    \*    \*    \*    \*    \*

His look, his breath had choaked her soul.    Death's
    hand
Had stiffened her fair tresses, and the grasp
Of his cold clammy fingers in their clasp
Mottled her beauty with damp mildewed stains.
That eye of beams is stagnant ; no more rains
The dew of pity on the buds below,
Which echoed with their sighs.    A dismal band
Of mourners is around, and sable woe
Clouds every feature.    Then the sullen knell
'Waked from its nest within the muffled bell,
And shadowy trains of black moved slowly on,
And priests shrouded their prayers in solemn tone.
He heard no more.    Away, away he flew—
Over the waves that roared, the storms that blew
The clouds that lowered, till the cave was nigh,
The fatal cave with its dun canopy
Of venomed mist.    He came ; the dark depths
    roared,
To welcome him to death : a curse he poured

That made the cold stones chatter, and the toads
Crawl, withered by his shrieks, from dank abodes
Where poison hatches reptiles.   Echo, bound
In mossy walls, oozed fear-drops at the sound,
But gave no answer.   Still his breathing seared
The slimy snake, that, on curled tail upreared,
Hissed forth its fright.   The waveless, stagnant well
Sunk deep, and hid within its muddy shell.

### XIV.

\* \* \* \* \* \*

The cloud of doom is coming.   Ocean spouts
Its depth of darkness forth, and night sweeps
    down
To blend her horrors with it ; onward blown
Foams the palled tempest.   Then upstands the sea
With all its host of waters loftily,
And bubbles shrieks of wrath, and vomits routs
Of carcases, twined round with monsters' scales
That suck the limbs down.   Spiked with lightning,
    sails
Fire, with its snaky tusks and muttering threat,
That peers into the skies ; its roots are set
Far, far below the fathomless abyss
Of the deep waters.   With a searing hiss
The enemies moved on.   Then Leopold sent
A roar of horror up into the sky,
While the sea foamed upon his feeble cry.

\* \* \* \* \* \*

The storm was hushed.   Men tell not where he
    went.

THE END OF THE THIRD FYTTE.

# MISCELLANEOUS POEMS.

## THE COMET.

THE eye of the demon on Albion was
    turned,
    And, viewing the happy, with envy he
    burned;
He snarled at the churches, the almshouse he cursed,
Till hate of their virtue his silence had burst:
"Why waves yonder harvest? why glitters yon tower?
My hate they despise, and they scoff at my power.
Then lend me assistance, ye elements dire,
Attend at my call, air, earth, water, and fire."
He spoke; and, lo! pregnant with flame and with
    pest,
The scorch of the blast his rough mandate confessed,
The flame of the typhus, the stifling damp,
And there rode the blast that will smother the lamp.
"In vain you command us; the heart-easing prayer,
And the sounds of the hymn, as they wind through
    the air,
Blunt the arrows of sickness which pestilence bear."

Then loud was the roar as the wind fled away,
Till earth trembled, and spoke from the regions of
    day:

" The shocks of my mountains roll cataracts back,
And from north to the south could the universe
    crack,
But the heart of the ocean I may not attack."

The thunder was o'er and the motion was still,
But the god of the waters thus murmured his will :
"All Europe my waves in a moment shall hide,
And the old world, and new, be swallowed by
    tide,
But the Albion isle shall my prowess deride."

The waves had sunk down, and the billows were
    hushed,
Ere the flame of destruction before him had rushed.
"Whole cities and empires have died at my blast,
So strong is my power, my rapine so fast ;
But Britain, unhurt, shall endure to the last."

In vain frowned the demon : " Still terror I'll try,
And the envoy of Yamen shall fleet through the sky."
But while virtue and justice in Britain remain,
The fire-brand of Yamen shall dazzle in vain.


## QUATORZAINS.

### I.

#### TO PERFUME.

EXQUISITE masquer, who dost changeful flit
  Upon the sun-hatched zephyr, basking now
In the broad light, 'mongst roses thou dost sit,
  On crimson throne, in the thorn-guarded bough,

Veiled by pink curtains, which will scarce admit
　To thine embrace the bee with velvet brow ;
Or, winged as incense, rising to the sun,
　A dove-like messenger thou bearest the prayer ;
Or dost alight where streamlets gently run,
　Gilding in dew adown the morning air ;
Or bashfully dost common notice shun,
　Dividing as a kiss the ruby pair,
　　Which the coquetting night-wind only sips :
　　Stay till I fetch thee from those mellow lips.


## II.

### THOUGHTS.

SWEET are the thoughts that haunt the poet's brain
　Like rainbow-fringed clouds, through which
　　　some star
Peeps in bright glory on a shepherd swain ;
　They sweep along and trance him ; sweeter far
Than incense trailing up an outstretched chain
　From rocking censer ; sweeter too they are
Than the thin mist which rises in the gale
　From out the slender cowslip's bee-scarred
　　breast.
Their delicate pinions buoy up a tale
　Like brittle wings, which curtain in the vest
Of cobweb-limbed ephemeræ, that sail
　In gauzy mantle of dun twilight dressed,
　　Borne on the wind's soft sighings, when the
　　　spring
　　Listens all evening to its whispering.

## III.

### A RIVULET.

IT is a lovely stream ; its wavelets purl
  As if they echoed to the fall and rise
Of the capricious breeze ; each upward curl,
  That splashes pearl, mirrors the fairy eyes
Of viewless passer, and the billows hurl
  Their sparkles on her lap as o'er she flies.
And see, where onward whirls, within a ring
  Of smoothest dimples, a dark fox-glove bell,
Half stifled by the gush encircling ;
  Perchance some tiny sprite crawled to that shell
To sleep away the noon, and winds did swing
    Him into rest ; for the warm sun was well
      Shaded off by the long and silky down :
      So I will save it, lest the elf should drown.

## IV.

### TO SOUND.

#### I.

SPIRIT, who steal'st from silence's embrace,
  Lending to mortal thoughts a powerful wing ;
Now marching slow with solemn pace,
  The broken cries of passion syllabling ;
Now gambolling, with sprightly grace,
  In ladies' voices as they sing :
How thou dost prison up in lovely wreaths
  The hearer's soul, like buds, whose folded leaves
Conceal their lusciousness in rosy sheaths.

How, when some hapless beauty, sighing,
    grieves,
Thou barbest every arrowed sigh she breathes,
  And giv'st a sting to sobs she quickly heaves,
    Till down our tears in trickling gushes roll,—
    Tears, the pure blood-drops of the wounded
      soul.

### 2.

Thou hangest up in the caverns of our ears
  Thy precious dew-drops, and our inmost souls
Echo thy beauty.  When the lightning sears,
  Clad in thy power the lowering thunder rolls,
The scornful laugh of elements.  Past years
  Thou mournest when the bell suddenly tolls;
And then thou load'st with iron tone the gale.
  Thou hoverest with a wing plumed with sweet
      notes,
Moth-like, around the chords where music's veil,
  A mist raised from tune's ocean, duskly floats;
Or, fountained in the heart of nightingale,
  With tide of murmurs swellest along her throat.
    Sweet soother of my senses, flutter near,
    Or sleep for ever in my charmèd ear.

### V.

#### TO NIGHT.

So thou art come again, old black-winged Night,
  Like an huge bird, between us and the sun,
Hiding, with out-stretched form, the genial light;
  And still, beneath thine icy bosom's dun

And cloudy plumage, hatching fog-breathed blight,
  And embryo storms, and crabbèd frosts, that
    shun
Day's warm caress. The owls from ivied loop
  Are shrieking homage, as thou cowerest high,
Like sable crow pausing in eager stoop
  On the dim world thou glutt'st thy clouded eye,
Silently waiting latest time's fell whoop,
  When thou shalt quit thine eyrie in the sky,
    To pounce upon the world with eager claw,
    And tomb time, death, and substance in thy
      maw.


VI.

A FANTASTIC SIMILE.

A LOVER is a slender, glowing urn
  On beauty's shrine, his heart is incense sweet,
Which with his eye-lit torch young love doth burn;
  Then from its ardour cloudy ringlets fleet,
That we call sighs, and they with perfume turn
  Upwards, his mistress' whisperings to meet.
The breezy whispers and the sighs embrace,
  Like pink-wing'd clouds mixing above the hill,
And from their lovely toyings spring a race
  Of tears, which saunter down in cheek-bank'd
    rill,
Silvering with sparkling coil the fair one's face ;—
  Twin dew-drops which her startled senses spill
    From violet's eyes, that hide their tender hue
    Deep-caverned in a fringèd lake of blue.

## VII.

### ANOTHER.

'TIS a moon-tinted primrose, with a well
  Of trembling dew ; in its soft atmosphere,
A tiny whirlwind of sweet smells, doth dwell
  A ladybird ; and when no sound is near
That elfin hermit fans the fairy bell
  With glazen wings, (mirrors on which appear
Atoms of colours that flizz by unseen,)
  And struts about his darling flower with pride.
But, if some buzzing gnat with pettish spleen
  Comes whining by, the insect 'gins to hide,
And folds its flimsy drapery between
  His speckled buckler and soft, silken side.
    So poets fly the critic's snappish heat,
      And sheath their minds in scorn and self-
        conceit.

## VIII.

### TO SILENCE.

HUGE, viewless ocean into which we cast
  Our passing words, and, as they sink away,
An echo bubbles up upon the blast ;
  Oh ! could thy waves but vomit in their play
Those unseen pearls which thou dost clasp so fast,
  And hang them at our ears washed in thy spray,
What endless stores our casket, memory,
  Would brood on, and enjoy !  But wherefore now
Dost thou engulph our talk, and floodest by
  Uphurling clouds upon our moody brow?

E'en when we dumbly muse sometimes a sigh
  Of bursting blossom, or hoarse groan from bough,
    Break through thy foam, like Venus, ocean-
      sprung,
  And to our ears upon the wind are swung.


## IX.

### TO MY LYRE.

My lyre ! thou art the bower of my senses,
  Where they may sleep in tuneful visions bound ;
These trembling chords shall be their breeze-kissed
    fences,
  Which are with music's tendrils warmly wound,
As with some creeping shrub, which sweets dispenses,
  And on each quivering stalk blossoms a sound.
My lyre ! thou art the barrèd prison-grate
  Where shackled melody a bondmaid sleeps,
And taunting breezes as her tortures wait :
  With radiant joy the hapless prisoner peeps
And sings delight, with freedom's hope elate,
  When some fair hand upon the surface sweeps ;
    And still she beats against the prison bars,
    Till silence comes and smothers her pert jars.


## X.

### TO POESY.

Sweet sister of my soul ! thou, that dost creep
  Gently into my bosom, and there lie
In converse with my spirit, and now weep
  And anguish it with kindly agony ;

Now draw it with thy lore, dreadful and deep,
   Through wild, appalling dreams ; then tenderly
Toy and change smiles : oh ! now I feel thee pour
   Into my breast thy gushing tears of sound,
And bury the sharp fang in my heart's core ;
   Now balm with thy sweet breath the throbbing
      wound.
Thou and my soul oft on thought's pinions soar,
   Clasping like dew-drops in a flower, around
     That cast their rainbow-eyed pale beams, and
     kiss
     And tremble in their loveliness and bliss.

## XI.

### A CLOCK STRIKING AT MIDNIGHT.

#### I.

HARK to the echo of Time's footsteps ; gone
   Those moments are into the unseen grave
Of ages.   They have vanished nameless.   None,
   While they are deep under the eddying wave
Of the chaotic past, shall place a stone
   Sacred to these, the nurses of the brave,
The mighty, and the good.   Futurity
   Broods on the ocean, hatching 'neath her wing,
Invisible to man, the century,
   That on its hundred feet, a sluggish thing
Gnawing away the world, shall totter by
   And sweep dead mortals with it.   As I sing,
     Time, the Colossus of the world, that strides
     With each foot plunged in darkness, silent
     glides,

**2.**

And puffs death's cloud upon us.   It is vain
  To struggle with the tide ; we all must sink,
Still grasping the thin air, with frantic pain
    Grappling with Fame to buoy us.   Can we
      think
Eternity, by whom swift Time is slain,
  And dragged along to dark destruction's brink,
Shall be the echo of man's puny words?
    Or that our grovelling thoughts shall e'er be
      writ
In never-fading stars? or like proud birds
  Undazzled in their cloud-built eyrie, sit
Clutching the lightning, or in darting herds
    Diving amid the sea's vast treasury flit ?
      Sink, painted clay, back to thy parent earth,
      While the glad spirit seeks a brighter birth.


## TO A BUNCH OF GRAPES

### RIPENING IN MY WINDOW.

CLUSTER of pregnant berries, pressed
    In luscious warmth together,
Like golden eggs in glassy nest,
Hatched by the zephyr's dewy breast
    In sultry weather ;
Or amber tears of those sad girls
    Who mourn their hapless brother ;
Strung closely on the glossy curls
Of yon fair shrub, whose zigzag twirls
    Clip one another ;

Or silent swarm of golden bees
    Your velvet bosoms brushing,
Dropped odorous from the gummy breeze,
Lingering in sleep upon the trees,
    Whilst summer's blushing ;
Or liquid sunbeams, swathed in net
    Spun by some vagrant fairy,
Like mimic lamps fresh trimmed and set
In thick festoons, with ripeness wet,
    Moonlight to carry ;
Or drops of honey, lately stolen
    From the hive's treasury,
Bubbles of light, with sweetness swollen,
Balls of bright juice, by breezes rollen,
    And bandied high.
I watch with wondrous care each day
    Your little spotted blushes,
Dyed by the sun's rude staring ray ;
And soon I hope you'll ooze away
    In sunny gushes.
Then shall ye, veiled in misty fume,
    In polished urn be flowing ;
With blood of nectar, soul perfume,
Breathe on our cheeks a downy bloom
    With pleasure glowing.


END OF VOL. I.

CHISWICK PRESS :—C. WHITTINGHAM AND CO., TOOKS
COURT, CHANCERY LANE.

49

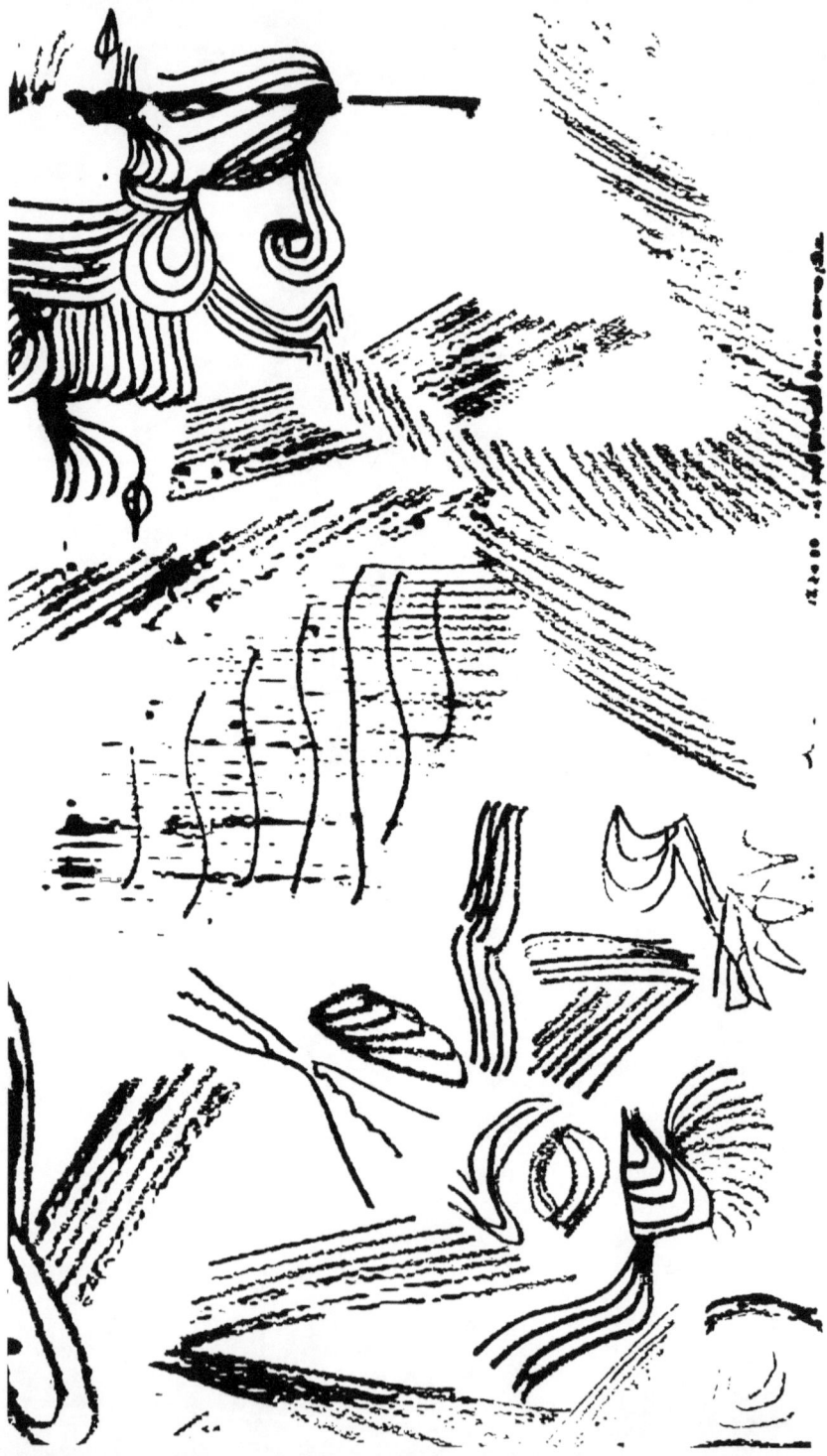

www.ingramcontent.com/pod-product-compliance
Lightning Source LLC
Chambersburg PA
CBHW031410270326
41929CB00010BA/1398